An Unfinished Church

An Unfinished Church

PAUL WASHBURN

A Brief History
of the Union
of
The Evangelical
United Brethren Church
and
The Methodist Church

Abingdon Press
Nashville

An Unfinished Church

Copyright © 1984 by Abingdon Press

Library of Congress Cataloging in Publication Data

Washburn, Paul, 1911-
  An unfinished church.

  Includes bibliographical references and index.
  1. United Methodist Church (U.S.)—History.
2. Methodist Church—History. I. Title.
BX8382.2.AW37   1984   287'.6'09   84-3098

ISBN 0-687-01378-X

Scripture quotations are from the Revised Standard Version of the Bible, copyrighted
1946, 1952, and 1971 by the Division of Christian Education, National Council of
Churches of Christ in the U.S.A., and are used by permission.

MANUFACTURED BY THE PARTHENON PRESS AT
NASHVILLE, TENNESSEE, UNITED STATES OF AMERICA

Dedicated
to Kathryn my wife
to Mary and Jane our daughters
to Fred and John
our sons

Contents

Preface

During my pilgrimage, lasting now for more than three score and ten years, I have become increasingly aware of God's grace coming to me through other persons who have been patient with me, have taught me, have tried to guide me, have inspired me, and have loved me. Most of these persons were gracious to me, not because of who I was, but because they had received grace from God through faith and were committed to sharing that grace so clearly demonstrated in the life, death, and resurrection of Jesus Christ. Consequently, Christian experience has never been only a personal experience for me, although it has had a personal dimension. There has been from the very beginning a communal dimension to my experience of the faith. In the Scriptures, I have met God through the experiences of ancient persons of faith. In prayer, I have been quite aware of other persons of prayer. In worship, I have been quite aware of other persons in congregations. In applications of the faith to social issues, I have witnessed the power of Christians who own life together.

I have loved beautiful church buildings, great organ music, enthusiastic singing of hymns, ardent prayers, magnificent anthems and solos in both minor and major keys, inspired preaching, and participation in the sacraments. I have responded to mature liturgies that always include the elements of worship and personal and social witness. All of this, and more, has kept me pondering the nature of the church. I understand, in part at least, the church as "the People of God," as "the New Creation," as "the Community of Faith," and as "the Body of Christ" but, alas, I still long for a more complete, a more excellent, experience of the church, not only for myself but for other persons of faith and for the world. I believe that many Christians sense values in the church which they have not yet claimed for themselves and that they yearn for acquaintance with and possession of those values. Surely, the claiming of these values is possible, but perhaps we will have to wait until the end of time to experience the ultimate fullness of the community of faith and "the grand amen."

I have written of my experience of the church as a life together with others in order to clarify my longtime interest in the ecumenical movement and the motivating force behind my work as the executive director of the Evangelical United Brethren Commission on Church Union (1964–1968). I worked consistently for a new church that was more than an institution but had an elaborate institutional dimension. This book was written with the desire to portray the church as the people of God in covenant with God and with one another, as Christian pilgrims on their way from the new birth to the ultimate realm and day of God and as a company of joyous servants in the world—helped often and hindered often by the weight of institutional baggage.

I express my gratitude to the Council of Bishops of The United Methodist Church for inviting me to write this brief history of the formation of The United Methodist Church. Much more could have been written of the faithful labors of hundreds of persons who negotiated and renegotiated portions of the Plan of Union. I express my gratitude to each and every one of them, many of whom have passed from the scenes of this life and have taken up residence in the land that is fairer than day.

The staff of the United Methodist Commission on Archives and History including Dr. John Ness, the Reverend William Beal, and Mrs. Suzanne Harlow greatly assisted me with the research.

Bishops Armin Härtel, Franz Shäfer, and Hermann Sticher and Professor Rudiger Minor from central and southern Europe provided valuable counsel in the formation of chapter 11, "Union Outside the United States."

Many helpful suggestions came from the Institute for the Study of Methodism and Related Movements of Garrett-Evangelical Theological Seminary at Evanston, Illinois.

Several bishops of The United Methodist Church read the entire manuscript, and Bishop Roy H. Short wrote a most generous foreword.

Mrs. Lucille Wilson typed most of the final copy while under the duress of many handicaps and much suffering, and Mrs. Robert (Gerda) Dahl retyped the final chapter. I am in their debt for their labors.

Kathryn, my beloved wife, read portions of the book as the writing progressed and made helpful suggestions for improvements, always encouraging me to be mindful of the feelings of persons mentioned in the book and to keep on keeping on.

Without the help of these persons, and the assistance of hundreds of persons who shared in the work of the formation of The United Methodist Church, not only this book, but The United Methodist Church could not have come to be.

November 21, 1983
Paul Washburn

Foreword

In *An Unfinished Church* Bishop Paul Washburn tells the story of the union of the Evangelical United Brethren Church and the Methodist Church that culminated in Dallas, Texas, in 1968. It is a long story including occasional conversations and sporadic negotiations dating back a century or more, but coming to a head between 1956 and 1968.

No one in United Methodism today is in a better position to relate this story, particularly of the events leading to the Uniting Conference, than is Bishop Washburn. Other persons gave strong leadership, such as Bishop Reuben H. Mueller, Bishop J. Gordon Howard, Bishop Lloyd C. Wicke, Bishop F. Gerald Ensley, and Dr. Charles C. Parlin, but no one person was more intimately involved in the final achievement of union than was Bishop Washburn. In 1964 the Evangelical United Brethren Church called him from the pastorate of First Church, Naperville, Illinois, and set him aside to work full-time on the union. As secretary he did much of the routine, wearying spadework of the Joint Commission. Many bishops have been elected as a result of some notable service for the church. The election of Bishop Washburn as the last bishop elected by the Evangelical United Brethren Church in its final General Conference was a high tribute to the appreciation that church felt for his significant service. The Methodist Church did not set aside a minister for a comparable responsibility, but a gifted layman, Doctor Charles C. Parlin, voluntarily gave his services with glad abandon in a similar role. Often in his work Bishop Washburn pays high tribute to Doctor Parlin.

Bishop Washburn tells the story of union in great detail—the various steps that had to be taken, the problems that had to be worked through, the difficulties that had to be overcome, the differences of viewpoint that had to be resolved, and the vast documentation that had to be prepared. The working documents that were necessary for the Uniting Conference bore the touch of the hands of Dr. Parlin and Bishop Washburn at almost every point. It is well that this detailed account has been preserved by the one person best in position to relate it.

In his book Bishop Washburn includes a great deal of background material, such as a lengthy discussion of the rootage of both the Evangelical United Brethren and the Methodist traditions in the Reformation. He also includes treatment of what for most United Methodists are forgotten chapters in the history of the establishment of a separate Methodist Church in Canada in 1828 and how this came about. He likewise treats the establishment of the Church of the United Brethren in Christ and the Evangelical Church in Canada, though that is a more recent story and a more familiar one. He explains in detail the efforts to encourage the Canada Conference and the Northwest Canada Conference to enter the union and the brotherly agreement to their going their own way when they did not choose to enter in. This chapter in United Methodist history could easily be forgotten had not Bishop Washburn chosen to record it.

Likewise Bishop Washburn treats at length the story of what union involved for both churches in middle and southern Europe. This is a story largely unfamiliar to most United Methodists. The bishop's treatment, particularly of the two episcopal areas in Germany and of the Geneva Area, is especially understanding and helpful.

All this is to suggest that there is a wealth of valuable material in the book in addition to the story of union itself.

The bishop's side comments are interesting and intriguing. Usually they are couched in a single sentence, but they are pertinent, arresting, and thought-provoking. They speak strongly of his commitment to ecumenism, to Christian unity, to full rights for women, to the recognition of minorities, and to justice for all.

The bishop brings the story up-to-date with an account of certain developments in the life of the church since union in 1968, particularly the development of the Doctrinal Standards statements, of the Social Principles, and of major changes in church structure.

As Bishop Washburn moves toward the conclusion of the book, he makes ten personal observations that are most interesting, with all of which some persons who have lived through the same period might not agree at every point, but that is, of course, to be expected.

While the bishop rejoices in the achievement of union and in any progress made since then, he remains unsatisfied and points pertinently to what he terms "the unfinished business of an unfinished church."

An Unfinished Church can be expected to find its place among the important records of United Methodism.

—*Bishop Roy H. Short*

1
Celebration of Union

Balmy spring breezes were blowing in Dallas, Texas, on the morning of April 23, 1968. By eight o'clock that morning, more than ten thousand members of the Evangelical United Brethren Church and the Methodist Church were gathering in the Dallas Memorial Auditorium to witness and to participate in the liturgy that sealed the union of their churches and marked the beginning of The United Methodist Church. They were gathered together from all over the world. Gathered with them were many fraternal delegates from other Christian churches. Dr. Albert Outler, the preacher of the morning, said in his sermon, "The eyes of the whole Christian community are focused on us and especially those of our Methodist brethren in Britain who are with us in spirit."

The moods of the assembled people were mixed. Some members of both churches were saddened at the thought of forsaking familiar ways of church life and at the prospect of the disruption of long-standing relationships. Others were exhilarated at the thought of sharing in the formation of a new church and at the possibility for new relationships. Whether they came with sadness or exhilaration or both, the liturgy molded the vast congregation into a community of Christians making covenant with God and with one another to be The United Methodist Church.

Because the Order of Worship within which the Evangelical United Brethren Church and the Methodist Church were united to form The United Methodist Church is one of less than a dozen such liturgies that have happened during this twentieth century, it is of utmost historical importance to include the full text of that liturgy at the very outset of this history of the union. What could be of greater significance than the record of what we said and did in the presence of God while bringing The United Methodist Church into being?

The Order of Worship

THE PRELUDE

Prelude and Fugue in E♭ major.................................J. S. Bach

Festival Fanfare on "Sine Nomine".......................Lloyd Pfautsch

THE PROCESSIONAL

For All the Saints..William W. How

For all the saints, who from their labors rest,
Who thee by faith before the world confessed,
Thy Name, O Jesus, be forever blest.
   Alleluia, Alleluia!

Thou wast their rock, their fortress, and their might;
Thou, Lord, their captain in the well-fought fight;
Thou, in the darkness drear, their one true light.
   Alleluia, Alleluia!

O may thy soldiers, faithful, true, and bold,
Fight as the saints who nobly fought of old,
And win with them the victor's crown of gold.
   Alleluia, Alleluia!

O blest communion, fellowship divine!
We feebly struggle, they in glory shine;
Yet all are one in thee, for all are thine.
   Alleluia, Alleluia!

And when the strife is fierce, the warfare long,
Steals on the ear the distant triumph song,
And hearts are brave again, and arms are strong.
   Alleluia, Alleluia!

From earth's wide bounds, from ocean's farthest coast,
Through gates of pearl streams in the countless host,
Singing to Father, Son, and Holy Ghost,
   Alleluia, Alleluia, Amen.

THE INVITATION TO OFFER THE UNION TO GOD

Dearly beloved, we are assembled here to unite The Evangelical United Brethren Church and The Methodist Church and thus to form The United Methodist Church. All here present are exhorted with eyes wide open to the mercies of God, and in the holy intention of love and obedience, to offer this union to God in the confident hope that it is acceptable to him and will be a blessing to his people.

In the grace of our Lord, Jesus Christ, let us go on to the perfection of our unity in him and in his Church.

THE CALL TO WORSHIP

This is the day the Lord hath made.

We will rejoice and be glad in it.

Blessed be the God and Father of our Lord Jesus Christ! By his great mercy, we are born anew to a living hope through his resurrection from the dead.

THE HYMN   † *The people standing*

Spirit of Faith, Come Down.............................Charles Wesley

Spirit of faith, come down, reveal the things of God;
And make to us the Godhead known, and witness with the blood.
'Tis thine the blood to apply and give us eyes to see,
Who did for every sinner die hath surely died for me.

No man can truly say that Jesus is the Lord,
Unless thou take the veil away, and breathe the living Word.
Then, only then, we feel our interest in His blood,
And cry, with joy unspeakable, "Thou art my Lord, my God!"

O that the world might know the all atoning Lamb!
Spirit of faith, descend and show the virtue of His name.
The grace which all may find, the saving power, impart;
And testify to all mankind, and speak in every heart.

Inspire the living faith, which whosoe'er receives
The witness in himself he hath, and consciously believes;
That faith that conquers all, and doth the mountain move,
And saves whoe'er on Jesus call, and perfects them in love. Amen.

THE INVOCATION   † *By the minister, the people standing*

Almighty and everlasting God, who has built thy Church upon the foundation of the apostles and prophets, Jesus Christ himself being the chief cornerstone; We pray thee to inspire the Church universal with the spirit of truth, unity and concord; and grant that all who confess thy holy name may abide in thy truth and live in unity and godly love; through Jesus Christ our Lord. **Amen.**

THE CALL TO CONFESSION   † *By the minister, the people seated*

Dearly beloved, the Scriptures move us to acknowledge and confess our sins before almighty God, our heavenly Father, with a humble, lowly penitent, and obedient heart, to the end that we may obtain forgiveness by his infinite goodness and mercy. Wherefore I pray and beseech you, as many as are here present, to accompany me with a pure heart and humble voice, unto the throne of heavenly grace.

THE CONFESSION   † *The people seated, bowed, and saying*

Our heavenly Father, who by thy love hast made us, and through thy love hast kept us, and in thy love wouldst make us perfect: We humbly confess that we have not loved thee with all our heart and soul and mind and strength, and that we have not loved one another as Christ hath loved us. Thy life is within our souls, but our selfishness hath hindered thee. We have not lived by faith. We have resisted thy Spirit. We have neglected thine inspirations.

Forgive what we have been; help us to amend what we are; and in thy Spirit direct what we shall be, that thou mayest come into the full glory of thy creation, in us and in all men; through Jesus Christ our Lord. Amen.

THE WORDS OF ASSURANCE   † *By the minister*

God loved the world so much that he gave his only Son, that everyone who has faith in him may not die but have eternal life. St. John 3:16

But should anyone commit sin, we have one to plead our cause with the Father, Jesus Christ, and he is just. He is himself the remedy for the defilement of our sins, not our sins only but the sins of all the world. 1 John 2:1, 2

THE LORD'S PRAYER

Our Father, who art in heaven, hallowed be thy name. Thy kingdom come, thy will be done, on earth as it is in heaven. Give us this day our daily bread, and forgive us our trespasses as we forgive those who trespass against us. And lead us not into temptation, but deliver us from evil. For thine is the kingdom, and the power, and the glory forever. Amen.

THE VERSICLE   † *The people standing*

O Lord open our lips.

And our mouth shall show forth thy praise.

Praise the Lord.

The Lord's name be praised.

THE PSALTER

O come, let us sing unto the Lord;

let us heartily rejoice in the strength of our salvation.

Let us come before his presence with thanksgiving;

and show ourselves glad in him with psalms.

For the Lord is a great God;

and a great king above all gods.

In his hand are all the corners of the earth;

and the strength of the hills is his also.

The sea is his, and he made it;

and his hands prepared the dry land.

O come let us worship and fall down;

and kneel before the Lord our maker.

For he is the Lord our God;

and we are the people of his pasture, and the sheep of his hand.

O worship the Lord in the beauty of holiness;

let the whole earth stand in awe of him.

For he cometh, for he cometh to judge the earth;

and with righteousness to judge the world, and the peoples with his truth.

Glory be to the Father, to the Son, and to the Holy Ghost;

As it was in the beginning, is now, and ever shall be, world without end. Amen.

THE EPISTLE   † *The people seated*

1 Corinthians 12:12–13:13

THE ANTHEM

I Will Extol Thee.............(Psalm 145:1–10).............Daniel Moe

THE GOSPEL   † *The people standing*

St. John 17:13–26

THE DOXOLOGY

THE NICENE CREED

WE BELIEVE in one God: the Father Almighty,
    Maker of heaven and earth,
    and of all things seen and unseen.

And in one Lord, Jesus Christ, the only-begotten Son of God,
    begotten of the Father before time began:
God from God, Light from Light, True God from True God,
    begotten, not made,
    one in essence with the Father,
    and through whom all things were made.
For us men and for our salvation he came down from heaven,
    and was made flesh of the Virgin Mary by the Holy Spirit,
    and became man.
He was crucified also for us under Pontius Pilate,
    he suffered and was buried.
On the third day he arose from the dead,
    as the Scriptures had foretold.
He ascended into heaven,
    where he sits at the right hand of the Father.
He will come again in glory
    to judge both the living and the dead,
    and His Kingdom will have no end.

We believe, in the Holy Spirit, the Lord,
    the Giver of Life,
    who proceeds from the Father and the Son.
Together with the Father and the Son
    he is worshipped and glorified.
    He spoke through the prophets.
We believe in one, holy, Catholic and Apostolic Church:
We acknowledge one Baptism for the forgiveness of sins:
We await the resurrection of the dead,
    and the life of the world to come. Amen.

THE SERMON

Visions and Dreams

"And in the last days it shall be, God declares, that I will pour out my Spirit upon all flesh, and your sons and your daughters shall prophesy, and your young men shall see visions, and your old men shall dream dreams;" Acts 2:17

THE HYMN   † *The people standing*

Jesus, We Look to Thee................................. Charles Wesley

> Jesus, we look to thee,
>   Thy promised presence claim;
> Thou in the midst of us shalt be,
>   Assembled in thy name:
>
> Thy name salvation is,
>   Which here we come to prove;
> Thy name is life and joy and peace
>   And everlasting love.
>
> We meet, the grace to take
>   Which thou hast freely given;
> We meet on earth for thy dear sake,
>   That we may meet in heaven.
>
> Present we know thou art,
>   But O thyself reveal!
> Now, Lord, let every bounding heart
>   The mighty comfort feel.
>
> O might thy quickening voice
>   The death of sin remove;
> And bid our inmost souls rejoice
>   In hope of perfect love. Amen.

THE SILENCE BEFORE THE OFFERING

O God, most merciful and gracious,
    of whose bounty we have all received:
Accept this offering of thy people.
Remember in thy love those who have brought it,
    and those for whom it is given,
    and so follow it with thy blessing
    that it may promote peace and good will among men,
    and advance the kingdom of our Lord Jesus Christ.

THE OFFERING OF THE UNION TO GOD

✝ *Then shall the ministers place the Holy Scriptures on the table.*

✝ *Then shall the editors of The Evangelical United Brethren Hymnal and of The Methodist Hymnal carry the hymnals to the table and place them side by side.*

✝ *Then shall the book editors of The Evangelical United Brethren Church and The Methodist Church carry the books of worship to the table and place them thereon side by side over the hymnals.*

✝ *Then shall the publishers of The Evangelical United Brethren Discipline and The Methodist Discipline carry the Disciplines to the table and place them thereon side by side over the hymnals and the books of worship.*

✝ *Then shall the secretaries of The Evangelical United Brethren Commission on Church Union and of The Methodist Ad Hoc Committee on EUB Union carry The Plan of Union to the table and place it over the hymnals, the books of worship, and the Disciplines as token that the two churches which lived under two books of law now become one church under one book of law.*

✝ *Then shall the chairman of The Evangelical United Brethren Commission on Church Union and the chairman of The Methodist Ad Hoc Committee on EUB Union read The Declaration of Union.*

THE DECLARATION OF UNION

I, REUBEN H. MUELLER, a bishop of The Evangelical United Brethren Church, hereby announce that the Plan of Union with The Methodist Church has been adopted by The Evangelical United Brethren Church in accordance with the procedures prescribed in its constitutional law, namely, by an affirmative vote of more than three fourths of the members of the Chicago General Conference present and voting on November 11, 1966, and by more than a two-thirds affirmative vote of the aggregate number of members of all the annual conferences in North America present and voting thereon.

I, LLOYD C. WICKE, a bishop of The Methodist Church, hereby announce that the Plan of Union with The Evangelical United Brethren Church has been adopted by The Methodist Church in accordance with the procedures prescribed in its constitution, namely, by vote of more than a two-thirds majority of the members of the Chicago General Conference present and voting on November 11, 1966, and by more than a two-thirds majority of all members of the several annual conferences present and voting thereon.

We now jointly declare that the Plan of Union between The Evangelical United Brethren Church and The Methodist Church has, by its terms and by the terms of the Enabling Legislation, become effective and henceforth The

Evangelical United Brethren Church and The Methodist Church shall go forward as a single entity to be known as The United Methodist Church.

† *Then shall Bishop Mueller and Bishop Wicke come, join hands over the Plan of Union, and say*

Lord of the Church, we are united in thee, in thy Church, and now in The United Methodist Church. **Amen.**

THE UNION OF THE MEMBERS

† *Then shall two children, representing all the children of the two churches, come, join hands over the Plan of Union, and say*

Lord of the Church, we are united in thee, in thy Church, and now in The United Methodist Church. **Amen.**

† *Then shall two youths, representing all the youth of the two churches, come, join hands over the Plan of Union, and say*

Lord of the Church, we are united in thee, in thy Church, and now in The United Methodist Church. **Amen.**

† *Then shall two adults, representing all the adults of the two churches, come, join hands over the Plan of Union, and say*

Lord of the Church, we are united in thee, in thy Church, and now in The United Methodist Church. **Amen.**

THE UNION OF THE MINISTERS

† *Then shall six ordained ministers, representing all the ordained ministers of the two churches on five continents, come, join hands over the Plan of Union, and say*

Lord of the Church, we are united in thee, in thy Church, and now in The United Methodist Church. **Amen.**

† *Then shall two church officers, representing all church officers of the two churches, come, join hands over the Plan of Union, and say*

Lord of the Church, we are united in thee, in thy Church, and now in The United Methodist Church. **Amen.**

THE UNION OF THE GENERAL CONFERENCES

† *Then shall the members of the General Conferences of The Evangelical United Brethren Church and The Methodist Church and all members of these churches present, stand, join hands, and say*

Lord of the Church, we are united in thee, in thy Church, and now in The United Methodist Church. Amen.

THE HYMN OF UNITY † *The people still standing*

All Praise to Our Redeeming Lord......................Charles Wesley

> All praise to our redeeming Lord,
> Who joins us by his grace,
> And bids us, each to each restored,
> Together seek his face.
>
> The gift which he on one bestows,
> We all delight to prove,
> The grace through every vessel flows
> In purest streams of love.
>
> He bids us build each other up;
> And, gathered into one,
> To our high calling's glorious hope,
> We hand in hand go on.
>
> We all partake the joy of one;
> The common peace we feel:
> A peace to sensual minds unknown,
> A joy unspeakable.
>
> And if our fellowship below
> In Jesus be so sweet,
> What height of rapture shall we know
> When round his throne we meet!

THE VERSICLE

The Lord be with you

And with thy Spirit.

Let us pray.

THE PRAYERS OF THE CHURCH

† *The minister will offer the prayers with the people responding.*

Almighty God, the Father of our Lord Jesus Christ: We give thee praise and hearty thanks for all thy goodness and tender mercies. We bless thee for the love which hath created and doth sustain us from day to day. We praise thee for the gift of thy Son, our Saviour, through whom thou hast made known thy will and grace. We thank thee for the Holy Ghost, the Comforter; for thy holy Church, for the Means of Grace, for the lives of all faithful and godly men, and for the hope of the life to come. Help us to treasure in our hearts all that our Lord hath done for us; and enable us to show our thankfulness by lives that are given wholly to thy service;

We beseech thee to hear us Lord.

O Lord Jesus Christ, who didst pray that thy Church might be one even as thou and the Father are one: Make us who profess one Lord, one faith, and one Baptism, to be of one heart and of one mind. Deliver us from blindness and prejudice, from intolerance and evil-speaking, that, joined in one holy bond of faith and charity, we, whom thou hast reconciled to thyself, may be reconciled to one another, and so make thy praise glorious; through the same thy Son Jesus Christ our Lord, who with the Father and the Holy Spirit liveth and reigneth ever, one God, world without end.

We beseech thee to hear us Lord.

We beseech thee, O Lord, to remember thy holy Church on earth; teach us to love thy house above all dwellings; thy Scriptures above all books; thy Sacraments above all gifts; the communion of saints above all company; and grant that, as one family, we may give thanks and adore thy glorious name; through Jesus Christ our Lord.

We beseech thee to hear us Lord.

Raise up, we pray thee, faithful servants of Christ to labor in the Gospel.

We beseech thee to hear us Lord.

We pray thee especially, heavenly Father, to bless our homes with thy light and joy. Keep our children in the covenant of their baptism, and enable their parents to rear them in a life of faith and godliness.

We beseech thee to hear us Lord.

Bless, we pray thee, the schools of the Church, universities and centers of research, all institutions of learning, and those who exercise the care of souls therein.

We beseech thee to hear us Lord.

Give to all men the mind of Christ, and dispose our days in thy peace, O God. Take from us all hatred and prejudice, and whatever may hinder unity of spirit and concord. Prosper the labors of those who lead and take counsel for the nations of the world, that mutual understanding and common endeavor may be increased among all peoples;

We beseech thee to hear us Lord.

We remember with gratitude those who have loved and served thee in thy Church on earth, who now rest from their labors. Keep us in fellowship with all thy saints, and bring us at last to the joy of thy heavenly kingdom;

We beseech thee to hear us Lord.

THE COVENANT † *The bishop presiding leading*

We are no longer our own, but thine. Put us to what thou wilt, rank us with whom thou wilt; put us to doing, put us to suffering; let us be employed for thee or laid aside for thee, exalted for thee or brought low for thee; let us be full, let us be empty; let us have all things, let us have nothing; We freely and heartily yield all things to thy pleasure and disposal.

And now, O glorious and blessed God, Father, Son, and Holy Spirit, thou art ours, and we are thine. So be it. And the covenant which we have made on earth, let it be ratified in heaven. Amen.

THE HYMN

Come, Let Us Use the Grace Divine.....................Charles Wesley

> Come, let us use the grace divine,
>   And all with one accord,
> In a perpetual covenant join
>   Ourselves to Christ the Lord.
>
> Give up ourselves, through Jesus' power,
>   His name to glorify;
> And promise, in this sacred hour
>   For God to live and die.
>
> The covenant we this moment make
>   Be ever kept in mind;
> We will no more our God forsake,
>   Or cast his words behind.
>
> We never will throw off his fear
>   Who hears our solemn vow;
> And if thou art well pleased to hear,
>   Come down and meet us now. Amen.

THE BENEDICTION † *By the bishop presiding*

The grace of the Lord Jesus Christ and the love of God and the fellowship of the Holy Spirit be with you all. **Amen.**

THE POSTLUDE

The Heavens Declare
   the Glory of God............(Psalm 19)........... Beneditto Marcello

† † †

THE PARTICIPANTS
(in the order of their appearing in the procession)

The Marshalls
> The Reverend Paul V. Church, Evangelical United Brethren Vice-chairman of the Commission on Entertainment and Program.

> The Reverend J. Otis Young, Methodist Chairman of the Commission on Entertainment and Program.

The Acolytes

Bearing the cross
> Mr. George Christian Engelhardt, Connecticut

Bearing the lights
> Miss Carolyn M. Hardin, Arkansas
> Miss Marlu Liwag Primero, The Philippines

Bearing the Scriptures
> Mr. Nobuhiro Imaizumi, Japan

Bearing the flags of the Church and the United States
> Mr. Quentin J. Faulkner, New Jersey
> Mr. John Felix Munjoma, Rhodesia

The Delegates from countries where the Uniting Churches Minister bearing flags of their countries

Algeria	Cuba	Korea	Puerto Rico
Angola	Czechoslovakia	Liberia	Rhodesia
Argentina	Denmark	Malaya	Sarawak
Austria	Dominican	Mexico	Sierra Leone
Belgium	Republic	Mozambique	Singapore
Bolivia	Ecuador	Nepal	South Africa
Brazil	Finland	Nigeria	Southern
Bulgaria	France	Norway	Congo
Burma	Germany	Okinawa	Sweden
Canada	Hong Kong	Pakistan	Switzerland
Central	Hungary	Panama	Taiwan
Congo	India	Peru	Uruguay
Chile	Indonesia	Philippines	Yogoslavia
Costa Rica	Japan	Poland	Zambia

The Councils of Executives and Secretaries

The Judicial Council

The Board and Council of Bishops

The Representatives Placing the Symbols of Union

Placing the hymnals
The Reverend Paul H. Eller, Editor of The Evangelical United Brethren Hymnal
The Reverend Carlton R. Young, Editor of The Methodist Hymnal

Placing the books of worship
The Reverend Emory Stevens Bucke, Book Editor of The Methodist Church
The Reverend Curtis A. Chambers, Book Editor of The Evangelical United Brethren Church

Placing the Disciplines
Mr. Lovick Pierce, Publisher of The Methodist Church
Mr. Donald A. Theuer, Publisher of The Evangelical United Brethren Church

Placing The Plan of Union
Mr. Charles C. Parlin, Sr., Secretary of The Methodist Ad Hoc Committee on EUB Union

The Representatives Offering the Union to God

Children
Miss Rhonda Elizabeth Renfro, Methodist child from Dallas, Texas
Master Robert O. Tupper II, Evangelical United Brethren child from Oklahoma City, Oklahoma

Youth
Miss Jean Boening, Methodist youth from St. Paul, Minnesota
Mr. Lester Kurtz, Evangelical United Brethren youth from Topeka, Kansas

Adults
Mrs. Emma Tousant, Evangelical United Brethren laywoman from Quincy, Massachusetts
Mr. J. P. Zepeda, Methodist layman from Fort Worth, Texas

Ministers
Evangelical United Brethren: The Reverend B. A. Carew of Sierra Leone, West Africa; The Reverend Merle A. Dunn, Rochester, Minnesota; The Reverend Herbert Eckstein, Berlin, Germany.
Methodist: The Reverend Paul A. Duffey, Dothan, Alabama; The Reverend Eric Mitchell, Bombay, India; The Reverend Roberto E. Rios, Republic of Argentina.

General Officers
Mrs. Porter Brown, General Secretary of The Board of Missions of The Methodist Church
The Reverend Harold H. Hazenfield, Executive Editor, Church School Publications of The Evangelical United Brethren Church

The Laymen Reading the Scriptures
   Mrs. D. Dwight Grove, President of the Women's Society of World
   Service of The Evangelical United Brethren Church
   Mr. Samuel L. Meyer, President of Ohio Northern University

The Ministers Conducting the Order of Worship
   The Reverend Paul Washburn, Executive Secretary of The Commission on
   Church Union of The Evangelical United Brethren Church
   Bishop Lance E. Webb, Chairman of The Commission on Worship of The
   Methodist Church

The Preacher of the Word
   The Reverend Albert C. Outler, Professor of Historical Theology at
   Southern Methodist University

The Bishops Declaring the Union
   Bishop Reuben H. Mueller, Indianapolis, Indiana
   Bishop Lloyd C. Wicke, New York, New York

The Bishop Presiding
   Bishop Donald Harvey Tippett, San Francisco, California

THE MUSICIANS PARTICIPATING

Organist—Mr. Phil Baker, Dallas, Texas

Director of combined choirs—The Reverend Carlton R. Young, Dallas,
Texas

School of Theology choirs represented in the combined choir

   Evangelical Theological Seminary, Naperville, Illinois
      The Reverend Eugene Wenger, Director

   Perkins School of Theology, Dallas, Texas
      The Reverend Carlton R. Young, Director

   Saint Paul School of Theology, Kansas City, Missouri
      The Reverend James Evans, Director

   United Theological Seminary, Dayton, Ohio
      The Reverend Aaron M. Sheaffer, Director

               The Reverend Norman L. Conard
                     Coordinator

Some prayers in this service adapted from
Service Book and Hymnal of The Lutheran Church in America,
adapted by permission of the publishers of the Service Book and Hymnal.

Dr. Outler's Sermon

Dr. Albert C. Outler, professor of historical theology in Perkins School of Theology of Southern Methodist University and an eminent and active ecumenist, was the preacher of the morning. His announced theme was "Visions and Dreams." His text was Acts 2:17: "And in the last days it shall be, God declares, that I will pour out my Spirit upon all flesh, and your sons and your daughters shall prophesy, and your young men shall see visions, and your old men shall dream dreams." But the sermon had a second theme with more poignancy in it. It was "The Unfinished Business of an Unfinished Church."

In his introduction, Dr. Outler related the birthday of The United Methodist Church to the first Pentecost and said, "In some ears, it may sound fantastic to relate this day to the first Pentecost recorded in Acts 2—what with no rushing wind, no tongues of fire, no glossolalia, and so forth. But actually, the lasting meaning of that Pentecost was its opening the way for others to follow after. . . . Clearly, though, that first Pentecost was less significant for what happened then than for what came after. Pentecost was the day when the real work of the church began, when Christian people accepted the agenda of their unfinished business in the world and began to get on with it."[1]

Suggesting that the formation of The United Methodist Church was only a limited reaching out toward the unity for which Jesus Christ prayed and that the documentation for the union left much to be desired, Dr. Outler said, "Obviously, no part of our venture in unity is really finished as yet. Our joy in this union ought to be tempered by our remembrance, in love, of those others of our Christian brethren, whom we acknowledge as such, and yet from whom we are still separated. Moreover, the various practical, domestic problems posed by our agenda in this Conference loom large and exigent. It will not be a debonair fortnight; few of us are likely to be content with the outcome. And yet, here we are and this is our birthday. Here we turn a new page in modern church history—and, just as smugness is excluded from our celebration, so also is cynicism."[2]

The outline for the main body of Dr. Outler's sermon was based upon the motto of the Consultation on Church Union which was and, thirty years later, is, "We seek to be a church truly catholic, truly evangelical, truly reformed." Was Dr. Outler, by adopting the Consultation on Church Union motto, suggesting that he would have preferred a more inclusive union? Perhaps he was, but I do not think he was. He was holding up ideals of Christian unity for United Methodists to see and heed, not only while they did the work of the Uniting Conference but as they lived their way through the forseeable future. The preacher knew that any true church would always have unfinished business and would always be, until the end of time, an unfinished church. So, his use of the motto was at the same time a way of prodding churchpersons to take to the ways of Christian unity and a valid description of every congregation and every church.

Truly Catholic

Dr. Outler described the meaning of being truly catholic when he said, "The basic meaning of the word 'catholic' is 'whole,' 'universal,' 'open.' It reminds us that true unity not only allows for diversity, it requires it. 'Catholic' has never really meant 'uniform,' 'lock-step,' 'produced by template.' It means 'inclusive'—a community in which all the members belong equally and by right of membership, in which all ministers share equally the basic office of representing the whole church, by right of ordination. It means 'open'—a community whose boundaries are set by the Christian essentials (the bare essentials at that) in which it is bad faith for anyone to deny full membership to any other save by the canons of faith in Christ and the Christian discipline that derives from that confession. This rules out all distinctions based on race, sex, class and culture—and so also all distinctions based on partisan emphases on this doctrine or that, this form of worship or that, this pattern of polity or that. . . . If we are to join in the search for a more inclusive, integral 'catholic' fellowship in this new church of ours the least we can do is to open our hearts and minds to yet further bold ventures in quest of Christian unity." [3]

Truly Evangelical

Holding that catholicity was not the only area of unfinished business, Dr. Outler called the new church to be truly evangelical. On this subject he said, "The church is called to mission, and her mission is both her message and the demonstration of that message in her corporate life. Her message is not herself either—it is her witness to the Christian Evangel: to the scandal and folly of Christ incarnate, Christ crucified, Christ resurrected, Christ transforming human life and culture, Christ in the world, Christ for the world; Christ in us, our hope of glory!

"Thus, the church we are called to be must be 'truly evangelical'—a church ablaze with a passion that God's Gospel shall be preached and heard and responded to in faith and hope and love by all who can be reached and instructed and gathered into the fellowship of God's covenanted People. The fullness of the Gospel embraces all human concerns everywhere and always; but the heart of the Gospel is startlingly simple: that God loves you and me and all men with a very special love and that Jesus Christ is the sufficient proof of this love to all who will receive and confess him as Saviour and Lord." [4]

Truly Reformed

But Dr. Outler's sermon proclaimed yet another dimension of required development. He said, "The church, even as she seeks to be truly catholic and truly evangelical, must also seek to be truly reformed."

In this portion of his sermon, the preacher conveyed the impression that the church must ever be open to reformation. He said, "A church truly reformed is one that is open, intentionally and on principle, to creative change of every sort (in teaching, discipline and administration)—not haphazard or reckless change but not timid and grudging, either. . . .Wherefore, now is the time, as at the first Pentecost, for young men to see visions and for old men to dream dreams—visions and dreams that ask more of the United Methodist people than we have ever asked before, visions and dreams that offer a richer, fuller life for all God's People, visions and dreams that see this 'new' church re-newed yet again and again, not only in the Spirit but in her structures, functions and folkways."[5]

I am not convinced that all the members of the new church or all the members of the Uniting Conference really heard Dr. Outler's impassioned plea for us to stand structurally and spiritually tall—in short, to do more than tinker with the church's machinery and to take seriously and functionally the roles to which he called the church. In a concluding paragraph the preacher said: "This, then is our birthday—a day to celebrate, a date to remember, a day for high hopes and renewed commitments. . . . Let us really rejoice and be glad in it—glad for the new chance God now gives us: to be a church united in order to be uniting, a church repentant in order to be a church redemptive, a church cruciform in order to manifest God's triumphant agony for mankind."[6]

It should be abundantly clear that the title for this book is derived from Dr. Outler's sermon, but I do not mean to imply by the choice of the title that the living church can ever be found without some unfinished business or that it can ever be anything but unfinished. It is the nature of Christ's church to have unfinished business and to continue in her unfinished state. But it is also the church's nature to be growing in grace and to be going on to perfection.

The Covenant of Union

At exactly 9:49 A.M. Bishop Reuben H. Mueller began his declaration that the Evangelical United Brethren Church had adopted the Plan of Union with the Methodist Church in accordance with the procedures prescribed in its constitutional law. Bishop Lloyd C. Wicke made a similar declaration in behalf of the Methodist Church. Then they said in unison,

We now jointly declare that the Plan of Union between the Evangelical United Brethren Church and the Methodist Church has, but its terms and by the terms of the Enabling Legislation, become effective and henceforth the Evangelical United Brethren Church and the Methodist Church shall go forward as a single entity to be known as The United Methodist Church.[7]

Bishops Mueller and Wicke, who had served the cause of union with distinction as chairpersons of the Joint Commission on Union, joined hands above a table upon which symbols of the uniting churches had been placed. The symbols were the hymnals, the books of worship, and the books of *Discipline* of the two churches. A copy of the Plan of Union had been placed over the other books. This last action proclaimed that The United Methodist Church had accepted the two hymnals and the two books of worship as aids for worship in the united church and that the Plan of Union had superseded the former *Disciplines* of the two churches. With hands joined, Bishops Mueller and Wicke spoke the Covenant of Union, saying, "Lord of the Church, we are united in thee, in thy Church, and now in The United Methodist Church." The assembled congregation responded with a doxological "Amen."

The Sharing of the Covenant of Union

In the process of the sharing of the Covenant of Union, it was spoken seven times. In each speaking of it, persons from the uniting churches intoned the words of it: first, Bishops Mueller and Wicke; second, two children; third, two youths; fourth, two adults; fifth, six ordained ministers from five continents, sixth, two general church officers; and finally, all the persons in that vast auditorium stood, joined hands, and said,

> Lord of the Church, we are united in thee, in thy Church, and now in The United Methodist Church. Amen.

Toward the conclusion of the celebration of union, Bishop Tippett led the assembly in offering John Wesley's covenant prayer. The concluding hymn chosen for the occasion was Charles Wesley's covenant hymn, "Come, Let Us Use the Grace Divine," but, alas, few seemed to know the hymn and few recognized the hymn tune. Consequently, the hymn was poorly sung. It was, perhaps, an omen not only of how the Uniting Conference, April 23, through May 6, 1968, would struggle to be a less unfinished church, setting out to get on with its unfinished business in church and world. There was, and is, however, mature realism in holding that the church will be unfinished and will have unfinished business until the rule and realm of God come at the end of time.

When the liturgy was ended, The United Methodist Church was inaugurated, and the union was an actuality that had been adequately celebrated.

2

Rootage in the Reformation

Theological thought patterns of the great reformers of the sixteenth and seventeenth centuries provided well-nourished root systems for the beliefs of the founders of the churches that united to form The United Methodist Church seven-tenths of the way into the twentieth century. Ideas traceable to Martin Luther, Ulrich Zwingli, John Calvin, Jacob Arminius, John Wesley, and others may be identified in the thoughts of Philip William Otterbein, Francis Asbury, and Jacob Albright.

Martin Luther

Martin Luther lived from 1483 until 1546. His teachings were prompted by his desire to reform the church that centered in Rome. One of his more poignant teachings is that salvation comes by God's grace through faith, not by merit or good works. In his treatise *Concerning Christian Liberty* he wrote:

. . . a Christian, being consecrated by his faith, does good works; but he is not by these works made a more sacred person, or more a Christian.[1]

Since then works justify no man, but a man must be justified before he can do any good work, it is most evident that it is faith alone which, by the mere mercy of God through Christ, and by means of His word, can worthily and sufficiently justify and save the person; and that a Christian man needs no work, no law, for his salvation; for by faith he is free from all law, and in perfect freedom does gratuitously all that he does, seeking nothing either of profit or of salvation—since by the grace of God he is already saved and rich in all things through his faith—but solely that which is well-pleasing to God.[2]

A Christian man is the most free lord of all, and subject to none; a Christian man is the most dutiful servant of all, and subject to everyone.[3]

In his treatise *Babylonish Captivity of the Church,* Luther challenged Rome with another poignant idea by saying that the sacraments were means of grace to bring individuals into right relationships to God: "The sole value of a sacrament is its witness to the divine promise. It seals or attests the God-given pledge of union with Christ and forgiveness of sins. It strengthens faith. Tried by the Scripture standard, there are only two sacraments, baptism and the Lord's Supper."[4]

In his *Address to the Christian Nobility of the German Nation,* Luther advocated the idea of the priesthood of all believers, saying, "We are all consecrated priests by Baptism, as St. Peter says: 'Ye are a royal priesthood, a holy nation' " (I Pet. 2:9). In that address the following defense of Luther's premise is found:

> We see, then, that just as those that we call spiritual, or priests, bishops, or popes, do not differ from other Christians in any other or higher degree but in that they are to be concerned with the word of God and the sacraments—that being their work and office—in the same way the temporal authorities hold the sword and the rod in their hands to punish the wicked and to protect the good. A cobbler, a smith, a peasant, every man, has the office and functions of his calling, and yet all alike are consecrated priests and bishops, and every man should by his office or function be useful and beneficial to the rest, so that various kinds of work may all be united for the furtherance of body and soul, just as the members of the body all serve one another.[5]

Ulrich Zwingli

Ulrich Zwingli lived from 1484 until 1531 and fostered the Reformation in Switzerland. From his teacher Thomas Wyttenbach of Basel, he learned of "the sole authority of Scripture, the death of Christ as the only price of forgiveness, and the worthlessness of indulgences."[6] In *The First Helvetic Confession* Zwingli said: "Canonic Scripture, the Word of God, given by the Holy Spirit and set forth to the world by Prophets and Apostles, the most perfect and ancient of all philosophies, alone contains perfectly all piety and the whole rule of life."[7]

On the subject of forgiveness in Christ alone, Zwingli wrote in *An Account of the Faith:*

> . . . there is no other victim for expiating sin than Christ (for not even was Paul crucified for us); no other pledge of divine goodness and mercy more certain and undisputable (for nothing is as certain as God); no other name under heaven whereby we must be saved than that of Jesus Christ (Acts 4:12). Hence there is left neither justification nor satisfaction based on our works, nor any expiation nor intercession of all saints, whether on earth or in heaven, who live by anything but the goodness and mercy of God. For this is the one, sole Mediator between God and man, the God-man, Jesus Christ.[8]

Zwingli also taught that the Lord's Supper is only a thankful remembrance of the sacrifice of Christ: "That the body of Christ in essence and reality, *i.e.*, the natural body itself, is either present in the supper or masticated with our mouth and teeth . . . we not only deny, but constantly maintain to be an error, contrary to the Word of God."[9]

Williston Walker in his *History of the Christian Church* contrasts the theological styles of Luther and Zwingli, saying, "Luther thought of the **why** of salvation relatively infrequently. Luther's interest was much more in the **how**. To Zwingli the will of God rather than the way of salvation was the central fact of theology. To Luther the Christian life was one of **freedom** in forgiven sonship. To Zwingli it was far more one of **conformity** to the will of God set forth in the Bible."[10]

John Calvin

John Calvin lived from 1509 until 1564. His intimate friendship with prominent persons earned for him a familiarity with and acceptance in polite society that few of the reformers experienced. He studied law and theology but was never ordained. His theology was well systematized.

Man's highest knowledge, Calvin taught, is that of God and of himself. Enough comes by nature to leave man without excuse, but adequate knowledge is given only in the Scriptures, which the witness of the Spirit in the heart of the believing reader attests as the very voice of God. These Scriptures teach that God is good, and the source of all everywhere. Obedience to God's will is man's primal duty. As originally created, man was good and capable of obeying God's will, but he lost goodness and power alike in Adam's fall, and is now, of himself, absolutely incapable of goodness. Hence no work of man's can have any merit; and all men are in a state of ruin meriting only damnation. From this helpless and hopeless condition some men are undeservedly rescued through the work of Christ. He paid the penalty due for the sins of those in whose behalf He died; yet the offer and reception of this ransom was a free act on God's part, so that its cause is God's love.

All that Christ has wrought is without avail unless it becomes a man's personal possession. This possession is effected by the Holy Spirit, who works when, how, and where He will, creating repentance; and faith which, as with Luther, is a vital union between the believer and Christ. This new life of faith is salvation, but it is salvation unto righteousness. That the believer now does works pleasing to God is proof that he has entered into vital union with Christ. We are justified not without, and yet not by works.

Since all good is of God, and man is unable to initiate or resist conversion, it follows that the reason some are saved and others are lost is the divine choice—election and reprobation. For a reason for that choice beyond the will of God it is absurd to inquire, since God's will is an ultimate fact. Yet to Calvin election was always primarily a doctrine of Christian comfort. . . . It made a man a fellow laborer with God in the accomplishment of God's will.[11]

Jacob Arminius

Jacob Arminius lived from 1560 until 1609. He taught a modified Calvinism, a position which later found favor with John Wesley.

Over against the Calvinist doctrine of absolute predestination, Arminius taught a predestination based on divine foreknowledge of the use men would make of the means of grace. Against the doctrine that Christ died for the elect only, he asserted that Christ died for all, though none receive the benefits of His death except believers. He was at one with Calvin in denying the ability of men to do anything really good of themselves—all is of divine grace.[12]

John Wesley

John Wesley lived from June 17, 1703, until March 2, 1791. His convictions reflected his lifelong membership in the Church of England and his acquaintance with the convictions of reformers such as Luther, Zwingli, Calvin, and Arminius. He taught the sovereignty of God, salvation by grace through faith, the universal availability of grace, the individual's freedom to accept or reject saving grace, sanctification as a gracious act of God toward the believer, and faith expressed in action.

There can be little doubt that Wesley was influenced by these reformers. As he taught ways of doing theology, he must have identified the works of the reformers, of Aquinas and Augustine, and of the church fathers and his membership in the Church of England as the influences of *tradition*.

The process of thinking through the faiths of others and the process of the formulation of his own faith must have been seen by Wesley as the influence of *reason*.

After Wesley's conversion at Aldersgate, he had ample justification for emphasizing the influence of *experience*.

Mr. Wesley looked beyond the theologies he knew about, beyond his power of reason, and beyond his profound spiritual experience to the *Scriptures* for the authoritative foundation of his personal convictions. "Wesley's faith goes back beyond eighteenth century England and sixteenth century Germany, beyond Aquinas and Augustine and the Church Fathers, into the soil of the Hebrew world: to the experience of a God-obsessed people, Israel, and to a unique man, Jesus Christ"[13] to whom the Scriptures testify.

John Wesley said, "Our main doctrines, which include all the rest are repentance, faith and holiness. The first of these we account as it were the porch of religion; the next, the door; the third, religion itself."

He saw Christian experience as a process which began with the new birth and continued by going on to perfection which means absolute surrender to God's will and purpose, total emancipation from the tyranny of self, personal and corporate action motivated by love, justice and the promises of God set forth in the Scriptures.[14]

One general and natural assumption has been that Otterbein, Asbury, and Albright derived their basic theological orientations from John Wesley. Philip William Otterbein was a scholar of high repute. He knew well six languages, including Latin, Greek, Hebrew, German, French, Dutch, and some English. He was well equipped for his labors at Herborn where "the faculty put strong emphasis upon the importance of holy living and took great interest in mission work and all forms of what we now call Christian social action and concern."[15] Otterbein's roots of faith were in Reformed theology and not exclusively in Wesleyan thought, although there was some intermingling of thought. "This assumption is only partially true because the Church of the United Brethren in Christ (1789–1946) and The Evangelical Church (1803–1946) shared common inspiration from German pietism with the Methodists (1784–1968) and grew up alongside of them instead of being branches or splinters from them."[16]

Francis Asbury encountered the Wesleyan emphasis for the first time when a Mr. Mather (one of Wesley's itinerant preachers) visited near Asbury's home. He was further nurtured by the master of the forge where he worked, a Mr. Foxall, who was a religious man interested in the Methodists. Following the conversion of his mother, Asbury began to itinerate among the Methodists and began to be a tireless pilgrim, a tender shepherd of souls, and a dauntless leader. It is not strange that when Wesley was looking for leaders to send to America he should choose Francis Asbury.

Jacob Albright, like Otterbein, began his Christian experience in other-than-Wesleyan associations. He was reared in a Lutheran home, but he was religiously indifferent. When the Albrights lost several children during an epidemic, Jacob was counseled and comforted by Anthony Houtz, a Reformed minister, by Adam Riegel, one of Otterbein's lay preachers, and by Isaac Davis, a Methodist class leader. He joined the Methodist class which met at the home of Isaac Davis. He said: "At this time I knew of no association or professed Christians who seemed to be more zealous and active, and whose discipline and regulations suited me better, than the Methodists. For this reason I united with them and found among them opportunity to receive great blessings and benefit for my soul."[17] There was profound impact of Wesleyan thought upon the life and work of Jacob Albright.

It can be said of Otterbein, Asbury, and Albright that the roots of their faith were in both European pietism and in Wesleyan pietism.

It has been noted that Methodism in the United States, while cognizant of the heritage in and from Britain, never looked wholly upon this inheritance as normative for America. . . . The European heritage, accordingly, became for American Methodism not only a treasured gift to share; it became also a living and continuing repository of faith and life enlightening the moral demand placed upon church and nation.[18]

The impact of European and Wesleyan pietism upon the organizers of the churches that now form The United Methodist Church is illustrated by an incident out of Otterbein's ministry.

When his congregation in Baltimore built a larger finer parsonage, Otterbein preferred to continue to live, like Zwingli, in a little four-roomed building he loved so well and asked that the rental of the new house be given to the poor. When they brought him materials for a new suit he gave it to a poor man across the street. Soon many persons made him the intermediary for the distribution of clothes and all sorts of things to the poor, even as Spener and Francke had done at the pietistic center at Halle.[19]

This brief piece on "Rootage in the Reformation" speaks of the streams of belief and conduct still available to The United Methodist Church.

3
Early Relationships

Mutual interest between the Methodist Church (founded in 1784), the Church of the United Brethren in Christ (founded in 1789), and the Evangelical Church (founded in 1803) began much earlier than the churches through friendships formed between Francis Asbury, Philip William Otterbein, Jacob Albright, and their associates. Of the three founders, Otterbein arrived on the American scene first, landing in New York on July 27, 1752, after a tedious, four-month voyage. Albright was the second of the founders to arrive; he was born on May 1, 1759, at Fox Mountain, about three miles northwest of Pottstown, Pennsylvania. Asbury was the last, arriving on October 27, 1771, after a voyage that lasted fifty-five days. What did these founders bring with them that made their mutual relationships prophetic of the eventual union of their movements?

Philip William Otterbein

Before leaving Germany, in response to a call to minister among German-speaking people in the New World, Otterbein was born into a minister's home, was well educated at Herborn, was ordained in the Reformed Church of Germany at Dillenburg on June 13, 1749, and had served as minister at Ockersdorf. Philip William Otterbein was born on the fourth day of June, 1726, in the little town of Dillenburg.

His father, "the reverend and very learned John Daniel Otterbein," was for a while rector of a Latin school in Herborn, and afterward an affectionate and faithful pastor of congregations in Fronhausen and Wissenbach. He died in 1742. Philip's mother, Wilhelmina Henrietta, was a woman of superior understanding and piety. He had five brothers and one sister. The brothers all obtained a thorough classical and theological education, and devoted themselves to the sacred office.[1]

The charge of "Pietism" had been laid at the door of the Otterbein family; and the facts that have come down to us favor the supposition that it was one of the few German families in which the influence of the revival of the preceding century, promoted by Spener and others, was still cherished.[2]

Otterbein's parents spared neither pain nor expense on his education. At Herborn, he completed all classical and theological studies required of candidates for the ministry. His studies included Latin, Greek, Hebrew, philosophy, and theology.

At age twenty-four he began his preaching and pastoral ministry. The following description of his preaching reveals much about the preacher:

His sermons were remarkable for their plainness, spirit, and evangelical power: and they occasioned both censure and applause. His more pious friends, while in heart approving of both the matter and the manner of his discourses, advised him, nevertheless, to moderate his zeal, and to use greater caution in reproof, in order that he might avoid the displeasure of those in authority, some of whom had felt themselves too sharply reproved for their sins, by the young preacher.[3]

Otterbein was one of six ministers of the Reformed Church of Germany who presented themselves to the Reformed Church of Holland to be examined and commissioned as missionaries to America. Candidates for the mission were required to be "orthodox, pious, learned, of humble disposition, diligent, sound in body, and eagerly desirous after, not earthly, but heavenly treasure, and especially the salvation of immortal souls."[4]

Otterbein's Aldersgate

Otterbein had an Aldersgate experience after arriving in America. John Lawrence, the historian, described the event in the following paragraph:

Not long after he came to Lancaster, and immediately after he had preached one of his most searching discourses, a member of his congregation came to him in tears, bitterly lamenting his sins, and asked advice. Mr. Otterbein knew that this man was a sincere inquirer after the way of life, and yet, until he had entered into that way himself, he felt incompetent to direct him. But the visit of this penitent brought him to a crisis. Looking upon him sadly, yet tenderly, he only said, "My friend, advice is scarce with me today." The seeker went his way, and Mr. Otterbein repaired to his closet, and there wrestled, like Jacob, until he obtained the forgiveness of his sins, the witness of the Holy Spirit of adoption, and was filled with joy unspeakable and full of glory! Thus after several years of earnest seeking for a higher spirituality, an awakened member of his own congregation, in tears, asking for advice, was made the means of causing him to press into the kingdom.[5]

Jacob Albright

The parents of Jacob Albright, Johannes and Anna, were immigrants from the Palatinate. They landed in Philadelphia on September 19, 1732. They had sailed from Rotterdam on the ship *Johnson* of the Holland American Line. Leaving Philadelphia, the Albrights moved northward along the Schuylkill River, finally settling near Pottstown.

Raymond W. Albright, a direct descendant of Jacob Albright, described the home life of the Albrights.

Undoubtedly these Germans of the Palatinate had had their hearts warmed to a deep religious interest, especially in relation to a high moral standard of living before they sailed to this land. The pietistic movement of Spener and Francke spreading from the University of Halle had swept rapidly over central and southern Germany. This is evidenced not only in the family of the Albrights, but also in numerous other groups like the Moravians, the Amish, the Dunkers, the Mennonites, the Seventh Day Baptists, and the United Brethren in Christ. All of these religious groups grow out directly from these Palatinates. Beneath the surface there was a splendid mystical pietism which quietly enriched the home lives of many of these early German immigrants. While overtly they remained loyal to their traditional faiths they secretly longed for religious leaders who would stir their souls and rouse them to high moral living.

In one of these pietistic German homes, Jacob Albright was reared. His family, like the others of his generation, was largely a unit unto itself. With great effort they cultivated their rocky farm, providing for themselves almost all the necessities of life, and having many delightful long hours together. In these hours of fellowship, the strength of character of John and Anna Albright was impressed upon their children.

When one seeks to understand how Jacob could later come to such a practical and morally controlling religious experience, it is impossible to trace it to any other root than to the excellent, unassuming and unpretentious, yet decidedly effective pietistic way of life constantly illustrated in his home.[6]

The Declaration of Independence was signed when Jacob Albright was in his eighteenth year. Because the Albright family had come to love this new land, Jacob and his brother John offered themselves for service. "Albright served as a member of Captain Jacob Wiltz's Seventh Company, Fourth Battalion, Philadelphia County Militia, which was organized at Pottstown in 1781. Jacob was the drummer of this company and his brother, John, was the fifer. They participated in the battles of Brandywine and Germantown."[7]

When he was twenty-six years old, Jacob Albright married Catherine Cope. They purchased forty-five acres of fertile farmland in the northeastern part of Lancaster County. In addition to farming, Albright manufactured tile for roofing and perhaps made bricks. One of his tile molds may be seen in the museum of the Commission of Archives and History at Drew University.

The Albrights united with Bergstrasse Lutheran Church near Hinckletown. Because of Jacob's evangelical zeal, he was dropped from the membership of that church. A history of the Bergstrasse Church carried the following account of Albright's dismissal.

During the pastorate of the Reverend Henry Moeller, 1790–1797, we find the name of the notorious Jacob Albright, among the communicant members of this congregation. He afterwards left the Lutheran Church and became a fanatic,—he connected himself with the Methodist Church, in the state of New York, whither, it is reported, he had fled to escape the arm of justice. Afterward he became the organizer of the German Methodists in various parts of Pennsylvania, formerly known by the name "The Albrights"—"The Albright People"—but later known by the name of Evangelical Association.[8]

Albright's Aldersgate

Albright had an Aldersgate experience also. He described that experience in his autobiography as follows:

I walked thoughtlessly in the path of life, rejoiced with those who rejoiced and thought little about the object of human existence, regarded not the duties of mankind, much less of Christians, lived as though the little span of duration would last eternally, and committed many sins for which God threatened severe punishment. In such a condition of heart, most persons seem to be happy, perhaps many also judged so of me, since I seemed to be contented and cheerfulness smiled on my countenance. Yet I was not really happy, and I do not believe that a person in such condition can ever be entirely happy. After the enjoyment of all the pleasures which only the world can offer us, there remains a void, an uneasiness in the back of the heart, which awakens a painful feeling—this is the mystical voice of conscience which embitters all forbidden pleasures and enjoyments. Real joy, genuine happiness occur only through the consciousness of duties fully performed. Oh! Often I hear the whispering of this mysterious voice and many a time it spoke so distinctly and loud and seemed to accuse me when I was guilty of a sinful act, when I left undone some good which lay in my path or when I was compelled to say to myself that I was disobedient to the rule of virtue and the commandments of my Creator. At first I gave but little heed to this illusion, conscience; but since I still paid attention somewhat to it, it repeated its admonitions constantly and more forcibly and the more attention I paid to it, the louder it spoke in my soul until I finally began to get an insight into my sinful state and almost seized a resolution to improve myself, yet this resolution remained only a plan and never came to realization.[9]

In 1790, the Albrights lost several of their children during an epidemic of dysentery. On several occasions Albright was miraculously saved from death. The experience of these tragedies and near-tragedies led him to his Aldersgate. He wrote:

In the place of carnality, came a holy love to God, his Word, and all his true children. Gradually every anguish of heart was removed, and comfort and the blessed peace of God pervaded my soul. God's spirit bore witness with my spirit that I was a child of God; one joyful experience followed another, and such a heavenly joy pervaded my whole being, as no pen can describe and no mortal can express.[10]

Francis Asbury

Followers of John Wesley had come to America before Francis Asbury. Robert Strawbridge, a colonist from County-Leitrim in Ireland settled in

Frederick County, Maryland, sometime between 1762 and 1766. A group of Irish immigrants from County Limerick arrived in New York in 1774. Among them were Philip and Margaret Embury, Paul and Barbara Heck, and Peter Switzer. The organization of Methodism, however, awaited the arrival of Francis Asbury.

Asbury was the son of Joseph and Elizabeth Asbury. He "was born in Old England, near the foot of Hampstead Bridge, in the parish of Handsworth, about four miles from Birmingham, in Staffordshire."[11] Passages selected from his journal depict Asbury's early life.

My father . . . and my mother . . . were people in common life; were remarkable for honesty and industry, and had all things needful to enjoy; had my father been as saving and laborious, he might have been wealthy. As it was, it was his province to be employed as farmer and gardener by the two richest families in the parish. (July 16, 1762) My mother's paternal descent was Welsh; from a family ancient and respectable, of the name of Rogers. She lived a woman of the world until the death of her first daughter, Sarah. (April 5, 1802) My lovely sister died in infancy; she was a favorite, and my dear mother being very affectionate, sunk into distress at the loss of a darling child. (July 16, 1792) Many were the days she spent chiefly in reading; at length she found justifying graces, and pardoning mercy. . . . For fifty years her hands, her house, her heart, were open to receive the people of God and ministers of Christ; and thus a lamp was lifted up in a dark place called Great Barre, in Great Britain. . . . As a "mother in Israel" few of her sex have done more by a holy walk to live and by personal labour to support, the Gospel, and to wash the saint's feet; as a friend, she was generous, true and constant. . . . There is now after fifty years, a chapel within two or three hundred yards of her dwelling. (April 5, 1802)

I was sent to school early, and began to read the Bible between six and seven years of age, and greatly delighted in the historical part of it. My schoolmaster was a great churl, and used to beat me cruelly. . . . My father having but one son, greatly desired to keep me in school he cared not how long, but in this design he was disappointed; for my master, by his severity, had filled me with such horrible dread, that with me anything was preferable to going to school. . . . I made my choice, when about thirteen and a half years old, to learn a brand new business at which I wrought about six years and a half; during this time I enjoyed great liberty, and in the family was treated more like a son or an equal than an apprentice. (July 16, 1722)[12]

Asbury's Aldersgate

Asbury, like Otterbein and Albright, had an Aldersgate experience. It is a record in Asbury's *Journal* over the date July 24, 1744.

Mr. Mather (one of Wesley's itinerants) came into those parts when I was about fifteen; and young as I was, the word of God soon made deep impressions on my heart, which brought me to Jesus Christ, who graciously justified my guilty soul through faith in his precious blood; and soon showed me the excellency and necessity of holiness. . . . At about seventeen I began to hold some public meetings; and between seventeen and eighteen began to exhort and preach. (July 24, 1744)[13]

These accounts of the early lives of Otterbein, Albright, and Asbury show that their personalities were nurtured in very similar, if not identical, circumstances. All of them had what may be called an Aldersgate experience.

Associates in America

Otterbein, though belonging to the German Reformed Church and cherishing friendship there, found his closest associates among the Mennonites in the persons of Martin Boehm and Christian Newcomer. Boehm and Otterbein met first on Pentecost Sunday in 1766 in Isaac Long's barn in Lancaster County. There, Otterbein listened to Boehm preach. At the close of the service, Otterbein went to Boehm and said, "Wir sind bruder" (We are brethren). Otterbein and Boehm were the first bishops elected by the Church of the United Brethren in Christ in 1800. Martin Boehm's son, Henry, became a Methodist preacher and was for a time a traveling companion of Francis Asbury. Later on, Christian Newcomer was elected a bishop also.

Albright's earliest associates were George Miller, who kept the minutes of the conference sessions, and John Dreisbach. In 1801 and 1802 Miller's records are very brief as recorded here:

In the year of our Lord and Saviour Jesus Christ, 1801, the Association added only a few to its number. Several persons sought and found grace unto the pardon of their sins, so that they knew and were assured that God was their reconciled Father through Jesus Christ.

1802—During this year twenty persons united with the Association. Among them was a young man named John Walter, who entered the work of the ministry under the direction of the Reverend Jacob Albright.[14]

John Walter became Albright's first assistant.

Asbury's associates by 1773 were Richard Boardman, John King, Joseph Pilmore, George Shadford, Thomas Webb, Abraham Whitworth, Richard Wright, and Joseph Yearbry who attended the conference. Robert Strawbridge and Robert William were absent. By 1784 when the Christmas Conference was held, there were eighty-three Methodist preachers in America. Thomas Ware wrote, "Among these pioneers, Asbury, by common consent, stood first and chief."

Relationships Between Asbury and Otterbein

Asbury met Otterbein in 1771, the year of Asbury's arrival in America; "and Asbury ever afterward, cultivated their acquaintance, and embraced every favorable opportunity to enjoy their society."[15]

The History of American Methodism reported on the relationship between Asbury and Otterbein:

In 1774 Otterbein became pastor of the Second German Reformed Church in Baltimore, which he served until his death nearly forty years later. Asbury was greatly impressed with Otterbein's ability and devotion. Otterbein for his part, admired Methodist discipline, and according to Asbury, "agreed to imitate our methods as nearly as possible" in the Baltimore church. When the United Brethren in Christ were organized in 1789, Methodist polity and discipline were embraced on nearly every point. Asbury regarded Otterbein as a father in Christ, sought his counsel on many occasions, and requested that he assist in the Christmas Conference consecration service. Preaching Otterbein's funeral sermon Asbury described him thus: "Forty years have I known the retiring modesty of this man of God; towering majestic above his fellows in learning, wisdom, and grace, yet seeking to be known only of God and the people of God."[16]

John Lawrence in his *United Brethren Church History* described another aspect of these relationships:

In nearly all the communities where the German language was spoken the United Brethren preachers preceded the Methodists, and were in advance of them several years; and when the Methodists, under the energetic superintendence of Francis Asbury, pushed their way into the German settlements and towns, the Brethren were the first to receive them into their houses, to welcome them as ambassadors of Christ, and to afford them opportunity and facilities for preaching the Gospel, and extending among them the kingdom of Christ. This they did gladly, because the Methodists preached, with power and much assurance, a living Gospel—a living and heart-felt religion—which they had experienced, and for which they had suffered no little persecution.[17]

Relationships Between Asbury and Albright

In 1796, Jacob Albright had been granted a license as a local preacher, or exhorter, in the Methodist Church. His quarterly conference membership was with the class of Isaac Davis near Hahnstown, Pennsylvania. Soon after being licensed, he began preaching tours and found it impossible to attend the regular quarterly meetings. His habitual absence from the class meetings, and especially the quarterly meetings, caused his name to be lifted from the Methodist roll.

There is a tradition that Albright and Bishops Asbury and Lee were on horseback on their way to a Methodist conference.

When they stopped at an inn to spend the night these men discussed the matter of working in the German language. Asbury and Lee were adamant in their opposition to such work. In the morning Albright saddled his horse and turned homeward, saying, "If there is no room in the Methodist Church to work in the German language and win the Pennsylvania Germans, I am going back to do that work."[18]

Bishop Asbury made a similar offer to John Dreisbach in 1810, but Dreisbach said to the bishop, "We consider ourselves called of God to labor principally among the German population, and that thus far our labors had not been in vain." The language barrier was a real reason that Albright's followers failed to unite with the Methodists.

The Evangelical Association was formally organized in 1803. Raymond W. Albright reports: "Upon Albright's death, George Miller completed the first *Discipline* and articles of faith, which, when they appeared in print in 1809, were almost identical with those of the Methodists."

Attempts at Union

During the intervening years between the founding dates of the three churches and the consummation of union in 1968, frequent conversations about union transpired. Three serious attempts at union are worthy of mention here. One of them occurred between the Methodist Episcopal Church and the Church of the United Brethren in Christ between 1809 and 1813. A second one was between the United Brethren and the Evangelical Association in 1813. The other one transpired between the Methodist Episcopal Church and the Evangelical Association between 1843 and 1871. All three churches pursued union, and all three failed. Those who aspired to union would await another way and another time.

Methodists and United Brethren

Christian Newcomer reveled in the good relationships existing between the Methodists and the United Brethren. He was an early ecumenist. On February 12, 1809, he wrote in his journal: "Brother Enoch George and myself lodged together at Brother G. Hoffman's. We rode together to Brother Guething's where we had a long conversation respecting closer union between the English and German Brethren." This conversation proved consequential.

As a result of the conference at Guething's, Mr. Newcomer attended in March following, the Methodist annual conference for the Baltimore district, which met that year in Harrisonburg, Rockingham county, Virginia. At this conference, a committee of five elders was appointed to confer with Brother Newcomer, and "ascertain whether any, and if any, what union could be effected between the Methodist Episcopal Church and the United Brethren in Christ."[19]

The committee met during the conference and made a recommendation thereto. Newcomer reported, "After mature deliberation and discussion on their part, I received from the conference, a letter, which I was to deliver to

William Otterbein, in Baltimore. And it was further resolved, that a member of their body should be appointed to attend our next annual conference, as a delegate."

Thirteen letters were exchanged between the negotiating churches; the last one was from the United Brethren to the Methodists, dated May 1, 1813. The first letter over the signatures of Bishops Francis Asbury and William McKendree lifted three issues: (1) We think it advisable, for your own good and prosperity, that each minister or preacher acknowledged by the United Brethren in Christ should receive from his conference a regular license that would introduce them to our pulpits and church privileges. (2) As we have long experienced the utility of a Christian discipline to prevent immorality among our people, we would earnestly recommend to you to establish a strict discipline that may be a "defense of your glory." (3) All those members among you who are united in such societies, or hereafter may be united, may be admitted to the privileges of class meetings, sacraments, and love feasts in our church, provided they have a certificate of their membership signed by a regularly licensed preacher in your church.

The letters exchanged were always courteous, but under the gracious words seethed a debate about discipline. How much? By whom administered? For whose glory? One historian reports:

This union was not destined long to flourish. The venerable patriarch in the Methodist Episcopal Church, Mr. Francis Asbury, who aided in forming it, and who rejoiced in it, went up to God on the 31st of March, 1816. Shortly after this, a prominent presiding elder, in his excessive zeal for Methodism, declared he would recognize the terms of union no longer, and that the members of the United Brethren church could have free access to Methodist love feasts and class-meetings on one condition only, and that was, by joining the Methodist Episcopal Church. . . . Brethren meetinghouses, and class meetings, and love feasts, remained as they are to this day, open and free.[20]

Evangelicals and United Brethren

In 1813, Bishop Newcomer, ever-ardent for the unity of the Body of Christ, visited the Evangelical Association Conference. During the conversations about union, five paramount issues were considered: (1) What name would the resultant church bear? (2) What rights will local preachers enjoy? (3) What will be done about foot washing at the love feasts? (4) What form will the itinerancy take? and (5) What will be the authority of the written *Discipline?*

This effort at union failed for two reasons. First, the commissioners from the United Brethren side were not authorized to make any binding agreements. Second, in the judgment of the Evangelical Association commissioners, the United Brethren were not yet sufficiently formed into a denomination. They lacked a printed *Discipline* and their itinerant system was in disarray.

Methodists and Evangelicals

Less than thirty years after the Methodist Episcopal Church refused to work in the German language, in August of 1835 they appointed William Nast as a missionary to the German-speaking people in Cincinnati. He was educated at Tübingen, converted in a Methodist quarterly meeting, chosen editor of *Der Christliche Apologete,* and became known as the patriarch of German Methodists. Nast took leadershp in seeking a union between the German conference of the Methodist Episcopal Church and the Evangelical Association.

Conversation began in 1840 when a delegation of Methodists attended the General Conference of the Evangelical Association and offered to extend to them periodicals and other publications in the German language.

The general conference of 1843 received a committee of fraternal delegates sent by the Methodist Church to bring a proposal for establishing close friendship between the two churches so they might lend each other aid, fight with better success against the enemies of the cross, and labor for the temporal and spiritual welfare of the neglected German people of this country.[21]

In 1867 William Nast and Jacob Rothweiler visited the General Conference of the Evangelical Association again. Mr. Nast summarized the previous conversations about union and proposed an organic union between the Methodist Episcopal Church and the Evangelical Association. The terms Mr. Nast stated were: "Your conference would remain and our Methodist German work would be swallowed up by yours, and you, being in the majority would control it, and your English work would be fused into ours." Bishop Esher's response was noncommittal.

Arguments for union turned toward union for the sake of mission by 1868. Union would (1) create the strongest German Protestant church in the United States, (2) provide new oppportunities to share Wesleyan theology, (3) infuse local churches with greater strength and better evangelistic potential, and (4) offer additional barriers to Romanism and German rationalism. Bishop Dubs of the Evangelical Association spoke in favor of union with the Methodists both in the United States and in Germany.

Nast and two other Methodists visited the Evangelical Association General Conference meeting in "The Old Brick Church" in Naperville, Illinois, in 1871. Nast made an appeal for consummation of the union. After much debate, the conference voted the union—thirty-eight in favor and thirty-seven against. Bishop Esher, who was presiding, ruled the majority insufficient for so far-reaching an action. Evangelical Association periodicals, *The Evangelical Messenger* (English) and *Der Christliche Botschafter* (German), printed a prophetic summary of the matter in their December, 1871, editions.

We could suggest that if it be God's will that The Evangelical Association and The Methodist Episcopal Church become one body, this action of General Conference will not prevent it, even if it had been intended to cut off all further overtures. Providence can quickly change aspects and hearts, as we have an example in the union of German into one empire. The Evangelical Association wants to know the will of God and follow it in this matter. She does not desire to run ahead nor remain behind the leading of the great Head of the Church, without whom we can do nothing.

Many other events that sound like overtures to union transpired in the early years, but perhaps this introduction to such happenings will serve to show that the urge to obey our Lord's prayer "that they all may be one" has been in our minds and hearts for a long time. Pray God it is still in our minds and hearts.

4

Experiences with Rifts and Reunions

It is interesting to note that from the times of the formations of the Methodist Episcopal Church in 1784, the Church of the United Brethren in Christ in 1789, and the Evangelical Association in 1803 not a decade passed without either a serious rift in one or more of these churches, a serious attempt at union between two or more of them, or a successful healing of rifts within them. The years between 1784 and 1968 have been punctuated with rifts of which to repent and with reunions over which to rejoice.

The seventh edition of the *Handbook of Denominations in The United States* describes eighteen Wesleyan churches stemming out of the Methodist Episcopal Church, two churches stemming out of the Church of the United Brethren in Christ, one church stemming out of the Evangelical Association, and one church stemming out of the Evangelical United Brethren Church. These statistics do not take into account the eight churches involved in the unions of 1922, 1939, and 1946. Such statistics vigorously support Dr. Outler's statement when he said, "Obviously, no part of our venture in unity is really finished yet."

Experience of the United Brethren in Christ

Issues that caused a rift in the Church of the United Brethren in Christ were (1) the rising tide of clergy and laity who believed that the laity should have a part in the business of both General and Annual Conferences, (2) the bitter struggle over whether church members should belong to secret societies, and (3) the amendment of the church's constitution. The revision of the constitution became the ultimate rifting factor. Daniel Berger in his history of the church says:

The liberals, as the progressive portion of the church generally had come to be called, saw in the adoption of the constitution a prospect for an escape from the extreme radicalism which had so long dominated legislation, and the hope of a broader and freer life for the church. The radicals saw in its adoption the doom of principles upon which many of them laid a larger insistence than upon any other feature of the church's life.[1]

When, on May 13, 1889, the official proclamation came from the bishops that the amendments to the constitution had been approved, Bishop Milton Wright (the father of the flying Wright brothers), with fourteen others who had previously voted against the amendments, left the conference. They contended that they were the original church. Years of litigation in civil courts followed. When the courts decided in favor of the parent church and against Bishop Wright and his followers, the dissidents formed the Church of the United Brethren in Christ (Old Constitution). In 1980 that church reported 28,035 members in 281 congregations. That church was invited to enter The United Methodist Church in 1968 but declined.

Experience of the Evangelical Association

The Evangelical Association met in its fifteenth General Conference in October, 1871, at Naperville, Illinois, just a few days after the disastrous Chicago fire. Another fire, however, raged between the pillars of the church, for the doctrine of holiness was causing dissension among the leaders. Raymond Albright wrote of those days: "Unfortunately that which had begun as a struggle between men with intellectual differences had, with a change of the personnel in official positions, degenerated into a struggle of personal rivalries. The ecclesiastical position of the young Bishop Esher and his interpretation of the powers of the episcopacy as well as doctrinal freedom led a number of other leaders to seek a way to check these somewhat extreme policies."[2]

At the General Conference of 1875, the persons who opposed Esher's autocratic manner and his ways of interpreting the *Discipline* realized that he would be reelected. This opposition group worked for the election of Bishop Rudolph Dubs, who was a more democratic spirit. Raymond Albright wrote, "That this rivalry in personal ambitions would lead to disrespect for the episcopacy and ultimately to disunion in the church was rather obvious to the leaders with clearest insight."[3]

The next twenty years were a period of growth and development, but divisive elements persisted over such issues as slavery, secret societies, forms of church government, and the powers of leaders, especially of the bishops.

What, shortly after the close of the Civil War, had begun as a theological debate between men of integrity and fine intellectual capacity degenerated during the next generation into a personal controversy between leaders of the church. While the real differences were not primarily theological, the division of loyalties was largely among the lines drawn by the theological controversy. At the turn of the closing decade of the nineteenth century, the spirit engendered on both sides of the controversy had risen to such a level that an open break in the church was the logical result.[4]

Although there were farsighted laymen who tried to prevent the break, it came in 1891. Bishops J. J. Esher and Thomas Bowman met the 1891

General Conference in Indianapolis, Indiana, and Bishop Rudolph Dubs and his minority group met in Philadelphia, Pennsylvania, contending that the seat of the majority conference had been illegally chosen. Albright said, "The saddest four years in the history of the denomination followed during which many longstanding friendships were severed and new lines of allegiance were formed."⁵ On November 30, 1894, at Naperville, Illinois, after losing many battles in civil courts, the followers of Bishop Dubs organized the United Evangelical Church, taking 36 percent of the members and 30 percent of the itinerant ministers of the Evangelical Association with them.

An exceedingly rare phenomenon in Church History is the fact that a goodly number of leaders in the Evangelical Church who saw the denomination divided between 1887 and 1894 were among the leaders who brought the Evanglical Association and The United Evangelical Church together again a generation later in 1922. Scarcely had the records of the last law suits, occasioned by the division, been printed before some far-sighted and unbiased souls began to dream that this separation must eventually be corrected by a reunion.⁶

During the process of reunion negotiations, the commissioners from both sides were careful to deal with the issues that created the struggle for power in the time of separation. They provided for the continuation of the polity and doctrine of both groups. The Articles of Faith of the Evangelical Association were retained. The articles on Regeneration, the witness of the Spirit, Entire Sanctification, and Christian Perfection were treated in a separate chapter. Restrictions were drawn around bishops.

On Saturday morning of October 14, 1922, the two churches, separated for a quarter of a century, were reunited. The celebration of union took place in the Mack Avenue Evangelical Church in Detroit, Michigan. Once again the spiritual sons and daughters of Jacob Albright were reunited into one body and one spirit but not all of them. A small minority of the United Evangelical Church, working primarily in Pennsylvania, Ohio, and Illinois, persisted in separation. They took the name "the Evangelical Congregational Church." In 1980 this church reported 28,840 members and 161 congregations. This church was invited to consider entering The United Methodist Church in 1968 but declined to do so.

Experiences of the Methodist Episcopal Church

Three strong black churches that were once within the Methodist Episcopal Church now bear witness to racist attitudes among Christians in the yesterdays and todays. They are separate and distinct because these churches have well-developed traditions and because racism still abides.

The African Methodist Episcopal Church was organized by Richard Allen of Philadelphia and Daniel Coker and Stephen Hill of Baltimore. Richard

Allen was one of the outstanding men of his day. He rose out of slavery to freedom and to the episcopacy of the African Methodist Episcopal Church. The *History of American Methodism* describes some of the indignities visited upon black Christians.

As early as 1786 there was friction between blacks and whites in St. George's Church in Philadelphia. The blacks were expected to take places near the walls, to occupy back seats, and they were the last to commune at the Lord's Table. After the gallery was erected in 1786, the black members were henceforth excluded from the main floor, being allowed to sit only in the gallery. Some were forcibly moved to their own particular section. Deeply offended when Henry Manley and another trustee of St. George's tried to pull Absalom Jones and William White from their knees while in the act of prayer, Allen at the close of the prayer led them out of the church on a Sunday morning in November, 1787, and others followed.[7]

On April 9, 1816, the African Methodist Episcopal Church was organized. "The word 'African' was to suggest the dignity and importance of the black man as a person and not to imply that the church was to be segregated for the use of people of African descent."[8]

. The African Methodist Episcopal Zion Church was founded as a separate and independent church in 1820 in New York City. Movement toward the formation of this independent church had begun in 1796 when their leaders petitioned Bishop Asbury to let them hold meetings separate from the whites. "The cause for their action was a feeling of general dissatisfaction with the way they were treated. Particularly unsatisfactory to the blacks was the fact that they were seldom permitted to preach to the whites. They also were prohibited from joining the Annual Conference as itinerant preachers."[9] The New York Conference of the Methodist Episcopal Church sought action by the state legislature to bring all Methodist churches under the regulations of its *Discipline*. William M. Stillwell, the pastor of Zion Church (the first church built for blacks in 1800), resisted this action by the New York Conference as another act of oppression of black Methodists. When the new church was formed, it took the name African Methodist Episcopal Church—Zion in honor of their leader's local church.

The Christian Methodist Episcopal Church, which was known until 1954 as the Colored Methodist Episcopal Church, resulted not from a rift in the Methodist Episcopal Church, South, but from an amicable agreement between black and white members of that church. In 1866 black members were rapidly deserting the southern church. In an effort to conserve the black members and to provide religious independence for them, the organization of a separate and independent black church was planned. Early in 1870 the first Annual Conference of the new church was held at Carthage, Texas.

The new denomination was organized on December 15, 1870, at Jackson, Tennessee. William H. Miles and Richard H. Vanderhorst were elected bishops. After "taking out and putting in such things as would be for the highest interest of the church," the Articles of Religion and the *Discipline* of the Methodist Episcopal Church, South, were adopted by the new church as their own.

The cultural and social importance of the independent black churches is not always understood. The creation of these churches was one of the most important consequences of emancipation and reconstruction. A contemporary historian says: "It meant religious freedom for the blacks for the first time in their history and opened up to black leadership at least one field of social endeavor. To this day not even the most reactionary Southern white challenges the right of the black to determine his own religious concepts."[10]

These brief descriptions have been included here because these churches represent historical divisions in the Methodist Episcopal Church and they represent the problem of racism which we have only begun to solve.

The formation of the Methodist Protestant Church in 1830 was a genuine division in the Methodist Episcopal Church—a division that was to endure for 109 years. The first sign of the rift appeared in a debate over how presiding elders were to be chosen. The reformers, of whom Nicholas Snethen was foremost, saw the issue clearly drawn. "It was a question of authority, whether it rested in the episcopacy or in the General Conference."[11]

The second sign of the rift was the lay representation movement. Snethen, who was strongly republican, insisted with the patriots that, "To secure the inalienable rights, governments are instituted, deriving their just powers from the consent of the governed." Bishop James Straughn wrote, "If the General Conference had acceded to the petition, asking only for lay representation and the right of trial, there never would have been a Methodist Protestant Church."[12]

On the first Tuesday of November, 1830, in Baltimore, the organization of the Methodist Protestant Church was completed with the following understandings:

There would be no episcopacy but general and annual conferences were to elect a president and other officers.

The general and annual conferences would have an equal number of ministers and laymen.

The annual conferences would adopt their own mode of appointing the preachers, who would have the right of appeal.

The right of property would be vested in the congregations.

There would be the right of fair trial of accused persons and of appeal.

There would be no interference with the right of private property according to the laws of the states involved (evidently a reference to the right to own slaves).[13]

The Methodist Episcopal Church was destined to suffer an even more serious division in 1844. At the General Conference meeting in that year, the Methodist Episcopal Church divided into two successor bodies—the

Methodist Episcopal Church and the Methodist Episcopal Church, South. Two issues combined to cause the rift: (1) the polity issue revolving around the nature and power of the episcopacy versus the nature and power of the General Conference, and (2) the slavery issue naturally separating northern and southern constituencies. These issues came to focus on Bishop James O. Andrew.

He by inheritance and his wife by recent marriage owned several slaves. Others were slaveholders. A Baltimore conference member had been suspended for having slaves.

The Committee on Episcopacy was instructed to ascertain the facts in the case of Bishop Andrew and report the results of its investigation the next morning. They found that the bishop did possess slaves and submitted a statement from him in explanation—that a mulatto girl had been bequeathed to him by an old lady; that he proposed to liberate her when nineteen years of age, but the law of the state did not allow emancipation; that the same was true also of a black boy; also that his wife possessed slaves in her own right.

The next day a resolution was offered: "That the Rev. James O. Andrew be, and he is hereby affectionately requested to resign his office as one of the Bishops of The Methodist Episcopal Church." This resolution was adopted by a vote of 111 to 69.[14]

Several attempts were made to resolve the issues without success.

In the meanwhile on adjournment of the 1844 session the southern delegates met to decide on future action. A recommendation went out to all conferences in slaveholding states to send delegates to a convention meeting at Louisville, Kentucky, in May, 1845. This body of sixteen annual conferences declared that under the provisions of the Plan of Separation all former authority exercised by the Methodist Episcopal General Conference be dissolved; that the sixteen annual conferences represented hereby constitute a separate ecclesiastical connection, based upon the *Discipline* of the Methodist Episcopal Church—except only in so far as verbal alterations may be necessary to distinct organization—and to be known by the style and title of the Methodist Episcopal Church, South.[15]

This breach was destined to endure for ninety-four years. The *History of American Methodism* summarized the rift in two sentences. "Although the division of Methodism would not likely have occurred without the slavery contest, it still remains true that the division did not occur solely due to the slavery issue. The disagreement over the nature of the general superintendency, while not the basic cause, became the occasion of the division of the Methodist Episcopal Church in 1844."[16]

The Long Road to Methodist Union

Bishop John M. Moore wrote a book under this title. One of his most profound insights was stated thus: "The idea of union by reunion, or merger, was forever laid aside. Unification by reorganization was acceptable."

Consequently, union and the desirability of union depended almost entirely upon the Plan of Union.

Bishop Moore observed, "The process of union . . . and genuine union is always a process . . . requires time for due consideration of all that is proposed, understanding of all issues and factors involved, patience with persons of confused if not conflicting and even opposing views, and courage to continue courses that will lead inevitably to just and proper goals in the spirit and way of substantial unity."[17] He went on to say,

The Plan of Union sets up a commonwealth of balancing bodies wherein no one shall be supreme except in its own field, but all shall have responsibility, in cooperation and coordination for the welfare of the entire church. For anyone to usurp chief control or for anyone to become weak and ineffective in the discharge of its constitutionally assigned responsibility is to break down the governmental structure by which a nation-wide and a world-wide church can hope to function with its greatest efficiency, reach and power.[18]

Bishop Moore saw clearly that union was not at base a biblical or theological problem but a problem of creating a church government of distributed powers, with checks and balances on those powers. The Methodist Protestant Church, though the smallest of the three churches seeking union, wielded influence all out of proportion to its size. In 1911, President Thomas H. Lewis of that church addressed joint Meeting on Union and listed certain provisions necessary to the new order: (1) equal representation of lay and ministerial members in the conferences of the church; (2) some way for Annual Conferences to participate in the selection of district superintendents; (3) some provision for reviewing appointments; and (4) election by local churches of their officials. Another massive contribution to the union process by the Methodist Protestant Church was its patient and concerned waiting for the two larger churches to resolve differences between them and to grow toward a spirit of reconciliation. One Plan of Union had been defeated in 1925. "After the defeat of the Plan of Union between the episcopal Methodisms in 1925 . . . Methodist Protestant men took up the whole question of union again in 1930 and began a movement that ended in the Uniting Conference of 1939."[19]

The final Plan of Union was created by the commissions of the three churches at a meeting held in Evanston, Illinois, in August of 1935. Benefiting from the labors of previous commissions, the new plan was quickly developed. It emphasized seven points: (1) The name of the new church would be "the Methodist Church"; (2) The church would have but one General Conference, which would be its highest legislative body and it would be subject to five restrictive rules; (3) There would be six Jurisdictional Conferences, five based on geographical divisions and one to include the black Annual Conferences in America; (4) There was to be equal representation of ministers and laymen in the General, Jurisdictional, and

Annual Conferences; (5) There was to be a Judicial Council related to the General Conference and the Council of Bishops as the Supreme Court of the United States is related to Congress and the presidency; (6) The episcopacy was to be retained, and the delegates of the Methodist Protestant church were authorized to elect two of their number to the office of bishop; and (7) the Articles of Religion were to be those historically held in common by the three uniting churches.

Concessions were required of all the uniting churches. Bishop Straughn outlined those concessions as follows:

—The Name—all churches had to yield heritage.

—The Methodist Episcopal Church had to yield by accepting the plan for Jurisdictional Conferences, by accepting equal representation of ministers and laymen, and by accepting the Judicial Council.

—The Methodist Episcopal Church, South, had to yield by accepting a single General Conference, by accepting a minority role in the General Conference, by accepting an adjustment which retained blacks as full members of the church, and by accepting equal representation of ministers and laymen in all conferences of the church.

—The Methodist Protestant Church had to yield by accepting episcopacy in authoritative and administrative roles, by surrendering the right of appeal on ministerial appointments, and by accepting "bulk" *{total}* control over its affairs.

Even with so much being required of the participating churches, the plan was affirmatively voted by overwhelming majorities in the three General Conferences and in the Annual Conferences.

The Uniting Conference was held in Kansas City, Missouri, from April 26 to May 30, 1939. Bishop John M. Moore delivered the Episcopal Message in behalf of all the bishops. In it he said: "The fraternal spirit may be expected to have full sway in this Uniting Conference. On the larger matters we are in agreement. Since we have never separated in faith, we have no theological discussions. . . . This Methodism is no fabrication of ambitious, selfish ecclesiastics. It is rather a flowing together of great streams going out to the same seas."[20]

A small remnant of the Methodist Episcopal Church, South, declined to enter the union. In 1980 the Southern Methodist Church reported 11,000 members in 169 congregations in Virginia and Texas.

The Evangelical United Brethren Church

Johnstown, Pennsylvania, was the site for the final General Conferences of the Evangelical Church and the Church of the United Brethren in Christ and for the first General Conference of the Evangelical United Brethren Church. On a sunny morning, November 16, 1946, the assembled delegates sang "Lead On, O King Eternal" as the processional hymn. Bishop John S.

Stamm, senior bishop of the Evangelical Church, presented Bishop A. R. Clippinger, senior bishop of the Church of the United Brethren in Christ. Bishop Clippinger read the Declaration of Union that brought the Evangelical United Brethren Church into being.

Professor K. James Stein of Garrett-Evangelical Theological Seminary says in his doctoral dissertation, "Thirty-four courtships reputedly transpired between the two denominations within a century's time."[21] The last stage of these courtships took on serious dimensions when leaders of the two churches met informally at a meeting of the Federal Council of Churches of Christ in America in Atlanta, Georgia, in 1922.

In 1933 Bishop Matthew T. Maze of the Evangelical Church spoke the following significant words to the United Brethren General Conference:

It is my very great pleasure to say to this General Conference that the Evangelical Church is ready to enter into negotiations with the Church of the United Brethren in Christ for the fullest possible spiritual and organic union, assuming, of course, that these negotiations will comprehend a careful and mutual study of spiritual and economic problems and a mutual willingness to make such unit adjustments as will make possible the greatest measure of efficiency for the united body.[22]

Differences in creedal formulations, in ministerial orders, in ecclesiastical life-styles, in institutions, and in stewardship needed to be negotiated.

The Evangelical Church's creedal formulations were nineteen in number, plus a lengthy statement on the Doctrines of Regeneration, Sanctification, and Christian Perfection. Origins of the nineteen articles can be traced to the Methodist Articles of Religion; George Miller had recommended to the Conference of 1809 the adoption of a German translation of the Methodist Articles of Religion with the addition of an article "Of the Last Judgment." The United Brethren creedal formulations, entitled the Confession of Faith, numbered thirteen and cannot be so readily traced to the Methodist Articles of Religion. From 1946 to 1962 The Evangelical and the United Brethren creedal formulations were both printed in the *Discipline.*

Ministerial orders were two, deacon and elder, in the Evangelical Church, but there was only one order, that of elder, in the United Brethren Church. This difference was resolved by authorizing only one order, that of elder, for the Evangelical United Brethren Church.

As to ecclesiastical life-styles, the United Brethren were more liberal and democratic than were the Evangelicals. Dr. Paul Eller, in his book *These Evangelical United Brethren,* said: "It is strange that the Evangelicals, having risen exclusively from a lay movement, should have so early become so ecclesiastical, while on the contrary, the United Brethren which had arisen around ordained clergymen should have moved so far in the congregational direction."[23] No amount of negotiation could resolve this difference. What was required was an intermingling of personalities from the two churches.

Institutional adjustments were resolved gradually. The United Brethren supported five colleges, one theological seminary, one publishing house, and a number of homes for children and the elderly. The Evangelicals supported three colleges, three theological seminaries (one of them in Reutlingen, Germany), one publishing house, and a number of homes for children and the elderly.

Stewardship problems were reflected in the economic conditions of the two publishing houses and the ministerial pension programs, but the problems were soluble.

The name "Evangelical United Brethren" was a simple combination of names of the two churches, but it would hardly do in 1984. It did not recognize our sisters in Christ.

Motivations frequently mentioned for the union were: (1) to be a partial answer to our Lord's prayer "that they all may be one," (2) to correct problems of duplication and rivalry, and (3) to relieve some of the economic pressure that was upon the churches with a vengeance. Also, unity was in order to witness and to be faithful in mission.

The Plan of Union was overwhelmingly adopted at all levels of voting, and the church prospered during its twenty-two years of existence.

Conclusion

The presentations in this chapter seem to indicate that church unions are not achieved through the writing of a modern creed nor do they resolve all the problems. Church unions, in order to be achieved, must address and negotiate the problems of authority and power. It is as Bishop John M. Moore said: "Church union is a problem of creating a church government of distributed powers with checks and balances on those powers."

5
From Exploration to Negotiation

In late November of 1946, seven years after the union that formed the Methodist Church and just a few days after the union that formed the Evangelical United Brethren Church, the modern trek toward the union that formed The United Methodist Church began. It was a trek that had to wend its way through fraternal relationships, through explorations, through negotiations, through the ferment of debate at the grass roots and at conferences, and finally through votes in General and Annual Conferences.

Bishop G. Bromley Oxnam, representing the Methodist Church, presented a fraternal address to that first General Conference of the Evangelical United Brethren Church. He spoke of hopes he harbored in his mind and heart for the union of all churches in the Wesleyan tradition. He said he had a letter in his pocket inviting the Evangelical United Brethren Church to explore the possibility of organic union with the Methodist Church but considered the presentation of the invitation inappropriate at that time.

In late 1956, Bishop George Edward Epp of the Evangelical United Brethren Church sent a letter to Bishop Frederick B. Newell of the Methodist Church asking, "Is it possible to open negotiations on a more formal basis?"

On December 13, 1957, bishops of the two churches, who were in attendance at a meeting of the National Council of Churches of Christ in the United States of America in St. Louis, Missouri, met to discuss the possibility of union. At the conclusion of the meeting, Bishops Newell and Epp and others observed that there was little difference between Evangelical United Brethren and Methodist doctrine and polity. Differences recognized and discussed were: (1) disparity in the number of members; (2) denominational names; (3) life episcopacy versus term episcopacy; (4) method of securing district or conference superintendents; and (5) the overlapping of publishing interests, colleges, seminaries, and other institutions. When the Joint Commissions on Church Union came to the negotiating table, they discovered all five of these issues, isolated in 1957, continued to be important issues.

The first joint meeting of the Commissions on Church Union held in

Cincinnati, Ohio, March 5–7, 1958, listed nine reasons why union should be pursued: (1) union is God's will for the churches; (2) theological positions are quite alike; (3) emphasis on human dignity and Christian social action is similar; (4) histories run along parallel lines; (5) common terminology is used in polity; (6) more effective ministerial education programs could be conducted; (7) petitions for union with the Methodist Church were submitted by Evangelical United Brethren Conferences in Illinois and Kansas; (8) there are potential economies in administrative costs; and (9) there could be a possible strengthening of witness and mission.[1]

The Joint Commissions decided to prepare a resolution for submission to the Evangelical United Brethren General Conference in 1958 and to the Methodist General Conference in 1960.

On September 3, 1958, one month prior to the meeting of the Evangelical United Brethren General Conference at Harrisburg, Pennsylvania, the commissions met in Dayton, Ohio. There the following papers were presented:

> *Common History of Methodist and Evangelical United Brethren Communions* by Daniel L. Marsh,
>
> *Our Common Theology* by Bishop Harold R. Heininger,
>
> *Our Polity—Similarities and Dissimilarities* by Bishop Reuben H. Mueller,
>
> *The Methodist Jurisdictional System—Does It Present a Possible Pattern for Union* by Charles L. Parlin,
>
> *The Ministry* by Bishop Glenn R. Phillips, and
>
> *Achieving Mutual Acquaintanceship and Understanding* by Bishop J. Gordon Howard.

One very significant consequence of this meeting was the resolute rejection by Evangelical United Brethren commissioners of the proposition that their church become an additional jurisdiction in the Methodist jurisdictional system.

Bishop F. Gerald Ensley presented the fraternal address at Harrisburg on Friday October 10, 1958. The record of that session includes the following account:

Bishop F. Gerald Ensley, who had been presented earlier to the General Conference, in a direct, forceful and pleasing manner set forth the cause of Christian unity and, in particular, the call to organic union among denominations that are seeking to bear witness to Christ in a broken world. He pointed out numerous ties that warm our hearts as followers of Albright, Asbury and Otterbein. He minced no words in reminding us of the obstacles that must always be faced in organic church union but pitched himself to a higher note as he repeated: "There is no barrier to the union of churches that loyalty to Christ cannot surmount."[2]

The committee of the General Conference on Church Federation and Union, of which the Reverend Paul Washburn was chairman and Mr. J.

Britain Winter was the secretary, was poorly attended but was able to recommend to the General Conference and gain approval of the following resolution:

Resolved, that the Commission on Church Federation and Union of The Evangelical United Brethren Church be and hereby is directed in the spirit of ecumenicity and in cooperation with the Commission on Church Union of The Methodist Church:
(1) To further study and explore the possible advantages and the potential problems involved in organic union with The Methodist Church and to report thereon from time to time through the church press; and in such other manner as it may deem advisable; and
(2) To continue exploratory conversations with the Commission on Church Union of The Methodist Church for the purpose of developing possible bases for union.[3]

Some of the Evangelical United Brethren leaders had hoped for permission to negotiate a Plan of Union but had to be content with permission to explore further possibilities. Permission to negotiate was not to be granted until the next General Conference.

Bishop Reuben H. Mueller presented a fraternal address to the General Conference of the Methodist Church on April 27, 1960, at Denver, Colorado. During his address, he said:

It is the opinion of our commissioners that the Methodist representatives were willing to move with more speed and were more generous in the discussions of possible solutions of problems than we had a right to hope for. It is my impression that, if the union between our two denominations depends on the commissioners, it would not take long to effect it.

Our bishops, in their message to General Conference in 1958, analyzed our problems in this connection in the following brief paragraph: "What is it that keeps churches of common doctrinal positions, similarity of polity and spirit, from uniting? The barriers are often theological differences, an honored history, tradition, and a sense of self adequacy, geographical separation, social and economic class distinction, a lack of true ecumenicity, fear of loss of treasured essentials, factionalism within churches, and the questions due to personal, social, economic and missionary divisions."

The Evangelical United Brethren Church is honor-bound to acknowledge the marks of Wesleyan faith and Methodist polity as they arose out of, and centered in a religion of vital personal experience through the forgiving grace of Jesus Christ, and the endowment of His living Spirit to equip us for right living within ourselves and in all relationships of the common life.

In closing let me say that we are interested in church union because we believe that God wills it. We believe that it is in the plan of God that the body of Christ—His Church—should be one. We believe that essential to such unity is the unity of the Spirit. But we also know that the spirit requires incarnation in a body and we believe that this oneness of Christ's people was ordained of God to be the declaration to the world that God the Father sent His Son into the world to save it.[4]

The Denver General Conference of the Methodist Church adopted, on April 29, 1960, the recommendation of its Commission on Church Union which said: "The members of the two commissions are agreed that the time has come to move forward with a drafting of a plan for organic union. It is hoped that this may materialize in time for presentation to the Evangelical United Brethren General Conference of 1962 and the Methodist General Conference of 1964."[5]

Dr. Charles C. Parlin addressed the Evangelical United Brethren General Conference meeting in Grand Rapids, Michigan. The evening of October 25, 1962, was designated Inter-Denominational Night. Dr. Parlin spoke with great precision and eloquence to the theme "Our Common Heritage." The entire address ought to be preserved in this book, but space will permit only a few quotations.

First, may I express gratitude, on behalf of my church and personally, that you in this great General Conference have so honored The Methodist Church and me by the invitation to address you on this Inter-Denominational Night.

It is good that spiritual kinfolk meet together. I propose to review the heritages of our denominations and the interesting and effective bonds of common belief and history, and our common concerns in the ecumenical movement of our day, which will forever bar us from being strangers one to the other.

Tonight, as we speak of our common heritage, six great souls emerge, which I name in the order of their birth:

> John Wesley [1703–1791]
> Martin Boehm [1725–1812]
> William Otterbein [1726–1813]
> Francis Asbury [1745–1816]
> Christian Newcomer [1749–1830]
> Jacob Albright [1759–1808]

These men were contemporaries and, as I hope to show, greatly influenced each other. Each was a pietiest, believed the Christian faith demanded a personal conviction to Christ and each rebelled against the formalism of his established church: Wesley and Asbury against the Church of England; Boehm and Newcomer against the Mennonites; Otterbein against the Old World Reformed Church; and Albright against the Old World Lutheran. For a study of these men and their working together there is an abundance of historical material. Wesley, Asbury and Newcomer left detailed diaries and journals; Boehm was written up in detail by his son, Henry; Albright has been covered in detail by one of his scholarly descendants. *{Otterbein ordered all of his papers to be burned before he died.}*

In the next portions of the address, Dr. Parlin relates the "union-promising" story of how these six men and their descendants have worked together from 1771 to the present time. He turned then to a discussion of the ecumenical movement as he perceived it, saying:

For our day the grouping of family churches is a movment which is discernible and realistic. Recently the Presbyterians had a two-way get together. Two years ago three Lutheran Churches came together to form The American Lutheran Church and this year four other Lutheran Churches to form The Lutheran Church in America. The

United Church of Christ represents a merger of two units, in part across confessional lines. Your unions of 1946 represented a merger of two units and the Methodist union of 1939 a merger of three units, just as within our family group the Evangelical United Brethren Church and The Methodist Church are having conversations.

Dr. Parlin concluded his address with this paragraph:

The Ecumenical Movement of today finds its motivation in a deep sense that it is God's will. With all our differences and diversities at New Delhi, we began each day together with Bible study. And we worshipped and prayed together and sat together through periods of silent meditation entreating God's guidance. I felt strongly that the Holy Spirit was with us and amongst us. As we face the tasks ahead we will be on a quest for truth. We will be together striving to achieve some visible form of a unity of those who "confess the Lord Jesus Christ as God and Saviour according to the Scriptures and seek to fulfill together our common calling to the glory of the one God, Father, Son and Holy Spirit." Together, in humility, we will seek to be His followers. As we face the tasks ahead we do it in the conviction that we are serving God's will.

Unlike the Harrisburg General Conference, where the Committee on Church Federation and Union could barely muster a quorum, the committee dealing with union at Grand Rapids was packed to the walls. It prayed much. It debated long. Finally, the Reverend Paul Washburn and the Reverend Joseph Yeakel, who were, respectively, chairman and secretary of the committee, were able to take the following resolution to the floor of the conference and secure its adoption:

Resolved, that this 40th General Conference of The Evangelical United Brethren Church, in session from October 23 to November 1, 1962, in Grand Rapids, Michigan, does hereby authorize its Commission on Church Union, in cooperation with the Commission on Church Union of The Methodist Church, to continue its studies, and if possible to prepare a Plan and Basis of Union for the uniting of The Evangelical United Brethren Church and The Methodist Church.[6]

The conference authorized the commission to co-opt additional persons to help with the work, to keep the denomination informed, and to present a report at the next General Conference, and it called upon the entire membership to make the negotiations toward union a matter of earnest prayer.

How long shall we say it took to move from exploration to negotiation? Shall we say it took from 1946, when Bishop Oxnam held up his hope, until 1962? Or, shall we say it took from 1771, when Asbury and Otterbein first met, until 1962? At any rate, the passage of that resolution by the General Conference of the Evangelical United Brethren Church put the Commissions on Church Union in a position to work diligently for union for the first time.

6

A Plan for a New Church

When the Joint Executive Committee of the Methodist and the Evangelical United Brethren Commissions on Union met in Chicago on December 14, 1962, it met under new circumstances. For the first time, commissioners from both churches had been authorized by their General Conferences to negotiate a Plan of Union. Bishop Glenn R. Phillips in his opening statement expressed joy over the action of the Evangelical United Brethren General Conference and said: "The Evangelical United Brethren Commission now is mandated to prepare a plan and basis of union and there should be no hesitation or reluctance to do so."

During the period of exploration, described in the preceding chapter, commissioners had frequently rehearsed the numerous justifications for pursuing union, and they had fully realized what the impediments to union were. It was during the period of exploration that the major dissimilarities between the two churches came into sharp focus: the names of the churches, 11 million members versus 750,000 members, bishops for life versus bishops for four-year terms, district superintendents appointed by bishops versus conference superintendents elected by Annual Conferences, contrasting ecumenical stances and performances, differences in world mission policies, contrasting theological emphases in both churches which met awkwardly across denominational lines in some places, and a church with jurisdictional conferences (including a jurisdiction based upon race) versus a church without such regional conferences. When examined critically, both the justifications for pursuing union and the impediments to union were predicated on conditions already extant in one or the other of the two churches about to negotiate a plan for a new church.

Questions like the following crossed the minds of some of the commissioners. How can we be faithful to the heritages of the negotiating churches and at the same time contemplate a *new* church? How can we deal responsibly with the churches we are trying to unite unless we take seriously their constitutional law, their confessions of faith, their social principles, and their polities? How can we continue uninterrupted the ministries of the two churches unless we show high regard for all ministers (lay and clerical) and their current ministering activities? Nevertheless, the Joint Commission frequently said or implied that it was making a plan for a *new* church.

Times, when the Joint Commission could expect official response to its work, kept gentle pressure upon the commission's working agenda. General Conference of the Methodist Church would meet in Pittsburgh in April of 1964. General Conference of the Evangelical United Brethren Church would meet in Chicago in November of 1966. It was already December of 1962. The Joint Commission had forty-seven months in which to produce a plan for a new church.

Membership on the two commissions during the period between 1962 and 1964 included the following persons:

Methodist Laypersons

M. W. Hyde, Indiana
John Jordan, New Jersey
Charles F. Marsh, South Carolina
C. Raymond Meyers, California
Charles C. Parlin, New York
R. E. Smith, Texas
Helen C. Waters, Maryland

Clergypersons

Lawrence E. Guderian, Oregon
Jolly B. Harper, Louisiana
Edwing R. Kimbrough, Alabama
Alvin J. Lindgren, Wisconsin
Sumpter M. Riley, Ohio
Norman L. Trott, Washington, D. C.

Bishops

Matthew W. Clair, Jr., Missouri
F. Gerald Ensley, Iowa
James W. Henley, Florida
Paul E. Martin, Texas
Glenn R. Phillips, Colorado
Lloyd C. Wicke, New York

Evangelical United Brethren Laypersons

William Fox, Pennsylvania
Herbert C. Gerster, Canada
Garland Hubin, Minnesota
Lawrence L. Huffman, Ohio
Torrey A. Kaatz, Ohio
J. Britain Winter, Maryland

Clergypersons

Cecil R. Findlay, Kansas
Charles E. Kachel, Pennsylvania
Paul E. Miller, California
Glen O'Dell, Indiana
John Sawyer, Virginia
Paul Washburn, Illinois

Bishops

Harold R. Heininger, Minnesota
Paul M. Herrick, Ohio
J. Gordan Howard, Pennsylvania
Hermann W. Kaebnick, Pennsylvania
Paul W. Milhouse, Missouri
Reuben H. Mueller, Indiana
W. Maynard Sparks, California

In a first attempt to address the work that lay before it, the Joint Commission appointed five committees with equal representation from both churches upon them. The committees' names and their officers were as follows:

Committee on Confession of Faith and Ritual
Bishop Harold R. Heininger, Chairman
The Reverend Jolly B. Harper, Secretary

Committee on The Ministry
Bishop F. Gerald Ensley, Chairman
The Reverend Charles E. Kachel, Secretary

Committee on Ecclesiastical Program and Organization
Mr. Charles C. Parlin, Chairman
The Reverend Paul Washburn, Secretary

Committee on Relationship Outside of the United States
Bishop Reuben H. Mueller, Chairman
Bishop Glenn R. Phillips, Secretary

Committee on Institutions and Properties
Mr. Lawrence L. Huffman, Chairman
Mr. Charles F. Marsh, Secretary

Persons bent upon planning for a new church resting upon the histories of ten predecessor churches needed to bring their best skills and efforts to the task, and they needed the assistance of God desperately, extremely, and superlatively. Consequently, the work of the commissioners progressed in an atmosphere of prayer and worship. Some moments of such worship linger in the memories of the participants. One such moment occurred on September 19, 1963, when Bishop Matthew W. Clair said eloquently:

We are living in a confused and turbulent period in human history. People everywhere are disturbed and are giving expression to an innermost desire for justice and righteousness. The church is becoming a part of this struggle and should have a part in it but the church is likely to lose sight of its responsibility as the arm of God revealed in Jesus Christ. There is fear that the church will conform to the world and accept the techniques and practices of the world. St. Paul warns against conforming to the world. We are likely to do things the way the world does them rather than as Christ would do them. We want the world to know that Christ is working through his church to bring about personal salvation and social redemption. If we allow ourselves to be used by Christ, then Christ will bring into the world that for which we work.[1]

On March 23, 1965, Bishop Reuben H. Mueller made a statement on the renewal of the church. He said in part:

Spiritual renewal does not come by re-organizing the details in the *Discipline;* nor does renewal come by breaking with the past. I feel that the very spirit in which these Church Union negotiations have been going on is evidence of spiritual renewal in our fellowship.

It is important that we do not think we are dealing only with ecclesiastical machinery. Something has to happen to us! Let us all keep in mind the place from which we started ten years ago when these negotiations began. At that time Bishop Newell made a statement that re-opened the negotiations. He emphasized the spiritual heritage of our churches: "Our concern is for the salvation of individuals. The Methodist interest in social concerns is not accidental. John Wesley gave close attention to helping the downtrodden. Our constituencies should know that spiritual goals are important to us."[2]

Dr. Norman Trott, president of Wesley Theological Seminary in Washington, D. C., led the opening devotional period on Wednesday morning, March 24, 1965. In his message, he contrasted the Holy Week "march" recorded in the Gospels with the present-day "march" from Selma to Birmingham in Alabama. He said, "Some of the parallels between the two marches are obvious . . . the singing courage of a great cause . . . the ultimate powers of truth, justice and love to overcome . . . the depravity of man and the indignity to which man is subjected in this world. It is hard to identify ourselves with the march of New Testament days unless we identify with the march of our own day."[3]

On September 8, 1965, Bishop Heininger read John Oxenham's poem "Break Down the Walls."

> Break down the old dividing walls
> Of sect, and rivalry, and schism,
> And heal the body of Thy Christ
> With anoint of Thy chrism.
>
> Let the strong wind of Thy sweet grace
> Sweep through Thy cumbered house, and chase
> The miasms from the Holy Place!
>
> Let Thy white beam of light beat in,
> And from each darkest corner win
> The shadows that have sheltered sin!
>
> Cleanse it of shibboleths and strife,
> End all the discords that were rife,
> Heal the old wounds and give new life!
>
> Break down the hedges that have grown
> So thickly all about Thy throne,
> And clear the paths, that every soul
> That seeks Thee—of himself alone
> May find, and be made whole!
>
> One church, one all-harmonious voice,
> One passion for Thy high employs
> One heart of gold without alloys,
> One striving for the higher joys,
> One Christ, one cross, one only Lord,
> One living of the Holy Word.[4]

On September 9, 1965, Bishop F. Gerald Ensley led the commissioners in "An Order of Worship for Christian Unity." One of the prayers within that order expresses the dominant mood of the commissioners at work.

God our Shepherd, give to the Church a new vision and a new love, new wisdom and fresh understanding, the revival of her brightness and the renewal of her unity, that the eternal message of thy Son, undefiled by the traditions of men, may be hailed as the good news of the new age: through Him who maketh all things new, Jesus Christ our Lord.[5]

The Ways of Negotiation

The commissioners discovered early on that they could not negotiate a solution to a vision, a dream, or even a new proposal. Such values were too dimly delineated, too cloudy, or too obscure. Negotiations had to deal with real conditions in the participating churches, and those real conditions were set forth most clearly in the books of *Discipline*. Bishop Roy H. Short proposed that the Plan of Union include nothing that was not already extant in either one or the other of the two books of *Discipline*. While Bishop Short's proposal was not followed slavishly, it did serve well every facet of negotiation.

Negotiation was in itself an interesting process. It involved the discussion of an issue until a tentative decision was reached. Next, that decision had to be reduced to writing. After the tentative decision appeared in written form, that document had to satisfy the commissioners as an adequate statement of their decision. Once the commissioners were satisfied, the particular document was approved and referred to the editorial committee for inclusion in the Plan of Union.

The printing and mailing of official documents was done by The Otterbein Press of Dayton, Ohio.

The Plan of Union

After much discussion in the Joint Commission on Union, a decision was made on December 13, 1963, to include the following in the Plan of Union:

Message from the Joint Commission
Historical Statement
Part I—The Constitution
Part II—Doctrinal Statements and the General Rules
Part III—Social Principles
Part IV—Organization and Administration
Enabling Legislation

Historical Statement

Bishop Paul N. Garber of the Methodist Church and Bishop Paul W. Milhouse of the Evangelical United Brethren Church were asked to write the Historical Statement. That statement may be found near the beginning of every *Book of Discipline* published since union in 1968.

Part I—The Constitution

Early on, the attention of the Joint Commission was called to the fact that the Methodist Church had a Constitution, which was in some way separate from *The Book of Discipline,* although it was printed in that book. The Evangelical United Brethren Church had Constitutional Law which was considered to be part of *The Book of Discipline.* A decision was made, late in 1963, to follow the Methodist way in this matter since the proposed Constitution for the new church included most of the elements in the Methodist Constitution plus many items in the Evangelical United Brethren Constitutional Law.

The new Constitution, like the Constitution of these United States, provided for three estates of government: the episcopacy resembling the executive branch, the conferences resembling the legislative branch, and the Judicial Council resembling the judicial branch. Powers of the church's government were assigned to the three branches with an attempt to put checks and balances around each of them. Dr. Charles Marsh, president of Wofford College in South Carolina, reminded the commissioners that some political scientists believed there should be a fourth estate in the federal government to be known as the administrative branch. If applied to the church, this branch would include all administrative and program agencies in the Constitution, making it much more difficult to modify those agencies and destroying almost entirely the idea of an effective broad Constitution. Dr. Marsh's suggestion held some fascination for persons bent upon renewal, but it was not employed.

Charles C. Parlin, chairman of the Committee on Ecclesiastical Program and Organization, presented the first draft of the proposed Constitution on July 3, 1963. Much time was spent discussing the document, but it was finally approved after some amending on December 13, 1963, and ordered printed for distribution to the Methodist General Conference before April of 1964. The Constitution proposed negotiated solutions to four of the major issues: the name for the new church, the protection of the smaller denomination, the nature of the episcopacy, and the method of securing district superintendents.

The Name

Paragraph 2 of Part II of the Constitution proposed the name of the new church to be "The United Methodist Church." Many Evangelical United Brethren felt a new name important to demonstrate a union rather than an absorption. Then, too, the name "the Methodist Church" proved to be unavailable legally everywhere in the world.

Evangelical United Brethren had substantial work in at least three countries where American Methodism had none. In Canada, two Annual Conferences of American Methodism joined with conferences stemming from British Methodism to form the Methodist Church that in 1925 became part of the United Church of Canada. There, the name "the Methodist Church" is the property of the United Church of Canada.

A similar situation exists in Nigeria, where the Methodist Church that stemmed from British Methodism has gone into the United Church of Nigeria. In Sierra Leone, where Evangelical United Brethren had a thriving conference, there is another body called the Methodist Church that stemmed from British Methodism. In all of these places, the name "The United Methodist Church" was available legally.

The United Methodist Church held promise of being the most united Methodism anywhere in the world.

Twelve-Year Rule

Restrictive Rule Six was designed to assure the smaller of the uniting churches larger representation than their numerical strength would guarantee. Methodists outnumbered Evangelical United Brethren fourteen to one. The restrictive rule guaranteed a ratio of seven to one in all agencies of the church, but it was hardly a granting of power to the smaller group. It was a gesture of good faith promising representation, and it was much appreciated by Evangelical United Brethren people. The rule was the longest sentence in the Plan of Union.

The General Conference shall not do away with the following rights, which are hereby defined: In order that The Evangelical United Brethren Church shall be assured of effective representation in The United Methodist Church it is agreed that at the level of the General Conference, Jurisdictional Conferences, and Central Conferences and on all boards and agencies at the Annual Conference, Central Conference, Jurisdictional Conference and General Conference levels, in every instance there shall be chosen, during the first three quadrenniums following union, at least twice the number of representatives coming from Evangelical United Brethren Church membership as the relative numerical membership in said particular Conference would indicate in relationship to the number of representatives coming from The Methodist Church, and further agreed that during such period every General Conference and Regional Jurisdictional Conference, and if practical every Central Conference and Annual Conference, board or agency regardless of size shall have at least one such representative; provided that this provision shall not be applied so as to give to representatives coming from The Evangelical United Brethren church a majority position which, except for this provision, they would not have; and further provided that in the German Central Conference during the first three quadrenniums following union the relative number of representatives coming from the former Methodist Church and the former Evangelische Gemeinschaft shall be equal.[6]

Provision was made for this rule to self-destruct at the termination of three quadrenniums.

Episcopacy

Two issues were paramount in the consideration of the episcopacy: the combining of the two episcopacies and the question of life episcopacy after election versus term episcopacy. Bishop Nolan B. Harmon drafted the paragraph which was accepted as the solution of the first issue. It is Article I in Division Three of the Constitution and reads as follows:

There shall be a continuance of an episcopacy in The United Methodist Church, of like plan, powers, privileges, and duties as now exist in The Methodist Church and in The Evangelical United Brethren Church in all those matters in which they agree and may be considered identical: and the differences between these historic episcopacies are deemed to be reconciled and harmonized by and in this Plan of Union and Constitution of The United Methodist Church and actions taken pursuant thereto so that a unified superintendency and episcopacy is hereby created and established of, in, and by those who now are and shall be bishops of The United Methodist Church; and the said episcopacy shall have such further powers, privileges, and duties as are herein set forth.[7]

The second issue about episcopacy was not essentially about life episcopacy versus term episcopacy. Both churches had life episcopacy in practice except in a very few instances. Ways of holding bishops accountable seemed to be the underlying issue, and it seemed to many of us that the Methodist system of the review of a bishop's performance by a Jurisdictional Committee on Episcopacy was a more mature way of dealing with bishops than forcing them to stand for reelection. There was never any willingness on the part of Methodists to compromise on this issue, and only a few Evangelical United Brethren showed interest in such a compromise.

District Versus Conference Superintendents

The right of a bishop to appoint district superintendents as opposed to an Annual Conference electing conference superintendents was resolved in two ways. As an adjunct to the twelve-year rule, Evangelical United Brethren Conferences were given the right to continue their practice as long as they remained separate. At rock bottom this issue had to do with the sizes of Annual Conferences. In the Evangelical United Brethren Church no Annual Conference had more than three conference superintendents. One day, during the discussion of this issue, Bishop Paul Martin pointed to the fact that some Methodist Annual Conferences have anywhere from twelve to sixteen district superintendents. He then asked, "How would election of super-intendents work in such circumstances?" Mr. Lawrence L. Huffman, publisher at The Otterbein Press, was one of the first to get Bishop Martin's message and to yield on the proposition to elect superintendents. Other Evangelical United Brethren commissioners followed quickly in yielding the point.

Two additional (and significant) paragraphs were added to the Constitution as consequence of events at the Pittsburgh Conference. They appeared among the amendments offered at the Chicago Conferences and represent first the commissioners' and then the General Conferences' firm stand on racism and ecumenicity. The paragraphs follow:

Inclusiveness of the Church—The United Methodist Church is a part of the Church Universal which is one Body in Christ. Therefore all persons, without regard to race, color, national origin, or economic condition, shall be eligible to attend its worship services, to participate in its programs, and when they take the appropriate vows to be admitted into its membership in any local church in the connection. In The United Methodist Church no conference or other organizational unit of the church shall be structured so as to exclude any member or any constituent body of the church because of race, color, national origin, or economic condition.[8]

The other paragraph is also important:

Ecumenical Relations—As part of the Church Universal The United Methodist Church believes that the Lord of the Church is calling Christians everywhere to strive toward unity and therefore it will seek, and work for, unity at all levels of church life: through world relationships with other Methodist churches and united churches related to The Methodist Church or The Evangelical United Brethren Church, through councils of churches, and through plans of union with churches of Methodist or other denominational traditions.[9]

How easy it is to draft excellent paragraphs for inclusion in a constitution and how difficult it is to marshall the lives of church members to give reality to the words. But the newness comes only in living out the words.

Methodist General Conference—1964

On December 13, 1963, the Joint Commission voted to send the Constitution containing the above proposals to the Methodist General Conference meeting in Pittsburgh, April 26 to May 8 in 1964.

Once again, Bishop Reuben Mueller presented the fraternal address to this conference, saying:

I believe in this Methodist-Evangelical United Brethren union so much that I am willing to say that even if we have to die in our present being, structure, program and procedures for the sake of Jesus Christ and His Church, let us die. This is a paradoxical pathway to new life. If church union is to take place, there will have to be some dying in order that the new may be born.

Here I come back to where I started, with the trend of Christian history and the spiritual wave of the future, I sincerely want my church to be a part of that movement. I do not want my church to stand on the street curb while the Christian advance marches past. I do not want my church to be selfishly introspective, trying to reserve its own religious experience for its own people and for no one else. I want my church to lose itself for Christ and His world mission in order that it may be found in

Him. If necessary, I am willing that my Church should die as a separate entity in order that it might live on a more significant, a larger, and a more spiritual way for the glory of Jesus Christ.[10]

The Pittsburgh Conference experienced one of the first of the modern confrontations. Scores of Methodists for Church Renewal demonstrated before the conference by marching to one section of the balcony and then back again. They were accentuating what was already a long-standing and heavy burden for the Methodist Church, namely, the elimination of the Central Jurisdiction and the racism which that jurisdiction exhibited. Under such circumstances, union with the Evangelical United Brethren Church could hardly be of primary importance, but it was discussed; objections were raised to some of the preliminary proposals. Finally, the conference voted:

(1) That union with The Evangelical United Brethren Church be approved in principle.
(2) That the Methodist General Conference be called in Special Session in November, 1966, at the time, and if practicable, at the place of The Evangelical United Brethren General Conference for the purpose of reviewing and acting on questions of church union.
(3) That the Plan of Union with The Evangelical United Brethren Church as presented, together with amendments and the record of General Conference discussion and debate be referred to the proper Commission for further study and discussion with The Evangelical United Brethren Commission on Church Union and the bringing of a perfected Plan of Union to the 1966 Special Session for review and action.
(4) If a Plan of Union is adopted by the requisite votes of the 1966 Methodist and Evangelical United Brethren General Conferences it shall immediately be sent to the Annual Conferences of the two churches for adoption.

Ad Hoc Committee on EUB Union

The 1964 General Conference created out of its former Commission on Church Union an Ad Hoc Committee on EUB Union and charged it with pursuit of the union. Members of that committee were:
Bishop Fred Pierce Corson
Bishop E. Gerald Ensley
Bishop Roy H. Short
Bishop Lloyd C. Wicke, Chairman
Bishop Friederich Wunderlich

the following additional clergypersons:
Claire C. Hoyt
Tracey K. Jones, Jr.
Walter Muelder

Sumpter M. Riley
Norman Trott
F. Thomas Trotter

and the following laypersons:
Mrs. Porter Brown
Leon Hickman
Theressa Hoover
Olin Oeschger
Charles C. Parlin, Secretary
Lovick Pierce.

This arrangement allowed for continuity of persons in the negotiations who had been with the movement for some time.

An Executive Director Elected

With November of 1966 only twenty-six months away, with numerous committees to meet and guide, with hundreds of pages of documentation to be processed, and with many Evangelical United Brethren either poorly informed or opposed to the union, the Evangelical United Brethren Commission decided it would employ an executive director.

Since this writer was so intimately related to this decision, permit me to relate a personal experience.

One late summer day I was taking Bishop Harold Heininger, my own bishop, to O'Hare International Airport after a meeting in Naperville. He said, "You know, Paul, we need a full-time executive for our Commission on Church Union." Since I had observed and participated in the work of the commission for six years, I had to agree. Then Bishop Heininger asked, "Who do you think should be asked to do this?" I suggested one or two persons, to which my bishop replied: "Paul, you must do this work." My chief duties were to be that of director and interpreter of the work of the commission. So, on Sunday, November 1, 1964, I left my beloved people of First Evangelical United Brethren Church in Naperville, Illinois, to take a journey the end of which no one could predict.

Part IV—Organization and Administration

Several commissioners, but chiefly Lawrence L. Huffman from the Evangelical United Brethren side, favored attempting to produce as complete a proposed *Discipline* as possible to the General Conferences of 1966. Seventeen committees were appointed to accomplish that end. The membership of those committees is of historic interest. Evangelical United Brethren committee persons are listed in the first column, Methodist committee persons in the second:

Committee on Confession of Faith, Articles of Religion, and General Rules
  The Joint Executive Committee

Committee on Preamble to the Constitution
  Bishop Heininger   Bishop Ensley
  Paul A. Washburn   Norman L. Trott

Committee on the Local Church
  Paul Miller, Secretary   Bishop Short, Chairman
  Paul V. Church   Sumpter M. Riley
  Warren Mentzer   Robert E. Goodrich, Jr.

Committee on the Ministry
  Bishop Sparks, Chairman   Bishop Ensley
  Wayne K. Clymer   Norman L. Trott, Secretary
  John R. Sawyer   Ernest C. Colwell

Committee on Conferences
  Paul A. Washburn, Chairman   Charles C. Parlin, Secretary
  C. R. Findley   Bishop Corson
  Bishop Mueller   Bishop Short

Committee on Judicial Administration
  J. Britain Winter, Secretary   Leon E. Hickman, Chairman
  Kenneth W. Hulitt   R. F. Curl
  Bishop Kaebnick   Richard Erwin

Committee on Temporal Economy
  Bishop Herrick, Chairman   Claire C. Hoyt, Secretary
  Harley E. Hiller   Bishop Paul Martin
  Cawley H. Stine   Edwin L. Jones, Sr.

Committee on Administrative Councils
  Bishop Milhouse, Secretary   Bishop Wicke, Chairman
  Wendell C. Bassett   Bishop Corson
  Paul V. Church   D. Trigg James, Sr.
  Bishop Mueller   T. Russell Reitz
  Elmer Yoder

Committee on Publishing Houses
  L. L. Huffman, Chairman   Lovick Pierce, Secretary
  Bishop Kaebnick   Mrs. Robert Owens
  Charles E. Kachel   Bradshaw Mintner

Committee on Board of Missions
  Bishop Heininger, Chairman   Mrs. Porter Brown, Secretary

World Division
  Fred Bollman   Tracey K. Jones

John F. Schaefer
Bishop Heininger

Dow Kirkpatrick
Bishop Wicke

National Division
Marlo N. Berger
Bishop Sparks
Wesley O. Clark

J. Edward Carothers
Bishop W. Ralph Ward
Monroe T. Stringer

Women's Division
Miss Marion Baker
Mrs. Paul E. Horn
Mrs. C. Newton Kidd

Mrs. Porter Brown
Miss Dorothy McConnell
Mrs. Glenn E. Laskey

Committee on Board of Education
A. Glen O'Dell, Secretary

Myron F. Wicke, Chairman

Local Church Curriculum and Editorial
A. Glen O'Dell, Chairman
E. Craig Bradenburg
Willard W. Schulz

Henry M. Bullock, Secretary
Bishop W. McFerrin Stowe
Leon M. Adkins

Colleges and Universities
Bishop Howard, Chairman
I. Lynd Esch
Arlo Schilling

Ernest Colwell, Secretary
Myron F. Wicke
Charles F. Marsh

Theological Schools
Charles E. Kachel, Secretary
Paul H. Eller
John R. Knecht

Walter G. Muelder, Chairman
Bishop Loder
Gerald O. McCulloh

Committee on Board of Evangelism
O. E. Schafer
Mrs. Charles Taylor
John R. Knecht, Secretary

Sumpter M. Riley, Jr., Chairman
Bishop W. Angie Smith
Harry Denman

Committee on Lay Activities
William M. Fox, Chairman
Donald App
Nordon C. Murphy
Leonard Sorg

Robert G. Mayfield, Secretary
W. Carroll Beatty
Rudolph Schiele
Clare N. Pettit

Committee on Christian Social Concerns
Bishop Kaebnick, Chairman
Cawley Stine
Wilmert H. Wolf

Miss Theressa Hoover, Secretary
A. Dudley Ward
Edwin E. Reeves

Committee on Hospitals and Homes
Torrey A. Kaatz, Secretary
William Messmer
Paul S. Wheelock

Olin E. Oeschger, Chairman
Bishop Alton
Benjamin H. Christner

Committee on Commissions
> Garland Hubin, Secretary   Bishop Ensley, Chairman
> John R. Sawyer   J. Wesley Hole
> Paul A. Washburn   Robert Uphoff

Committee on Churches Outside the United States
> Bishop Mueller, Chairman   Charles C. Parlin, Secretary
> Herbert Gerster, Canada   Bishop Corson
> John F. Schaefer   Bishop Raines
> C. Zaiser, Germany   Bishop Wunderlich, Germany

All of these committees were given specific instructions as to their patterns of work:

1. They were to have at hand a copy of the Constitution, copies of the *Disciplines* of both churches, and reports of previous studies. Duties assigned to the agencies of the churches by the *Disciplines* constituted the current missions of those agencies.
2. They were responsible for formulating and drafting for the proposed *Discipline* portions that were assigned to them.
3. They were expected to base their recommendations for the united church upon provisions set forth in either one or the other of the present *Disciplines*.
4. They were expected to involve boards and agencies of both churches and the executives of such boards and agencies within the purview of the committee's work at the earliest possible date.
5. They were requested to submit copies of their drafted conclusions to the executive directors of the Joint Commission on Union.
6. They were requested to develop a work schedule that would make it possible for them to conclude their work by November 1, 1965.
7. Problem areas were to be referred immediately to the Joint Commission on Church Union. Fortunately, there were few such referrals.

Two new agencies resulted from the work of the Joint Commission and the seventeen committees: the Commission on Ecumenical Affairs and the Council on Ministries.

Commission on Ecumenical Affairs

A paper drafted by Paul Washburn entitled "The United Methodist Church and The Whole Church" was proposed, in the first instance, as a new Division Six for the Constitution under the heading "The Council of Interpretation." It was agreed that the detailed provision for the proposed council would not appear in the Constitution, but there would appear a brief statement in the Constitution and a detailed statement, including provisions for an ecumenical agency, elsewhere in the *Discipline*. The brief statement in the *Discipline* appears even now as Article V, Division One of the Constitution and, as will be revealed later, was the cause of much controversy in the 1966 General Conferences.

The name "Council of Interpretation" was changed by action of the commissioners to the "Commission on Ecumenical Affairs." Prior to the Methodist General Conference in 1964, some Methodist ecumenists were planning for such an agency, so the Methodist Commission on Union petitioned the Pittsburgh General Conference to create a Commission on Ecumenical Affairs. That petition gained approval, and the venture in church union bore fruit four years before union was consummated.

Council on Ministries

The Methodist Church operated with a number of administrative agencies: the Council of Bishops, the Council on World Service and Finance, the Council of Secretaries, the Interboard Council, and eight other interboard committees. The Evangelical United Brethren Church operated through the Board of Bishops and an Administrative Council. The Administrative Council had authority to act for the church in interims between General Conference sessions in cases of declared emergencies. A Program Council functioned as part of that Administrative Council.

One evident need in planning for the new church was an agency to coordinate program agencies. Much confusion existed in the Methodist Church between the Council of Secretaries, the Interboard Council, and the eight interboard committees. With Dr. Paul Church, executive secretary of the Evangelical United Brethren Administrative Council, leading the way, this need was largely met. At first the new council was called the Coordinating Council, then it was called the Program Council, and finally, after restructure in 1972, the Council on Ministries. The conception of this council was the greatest structural gift the Evangelical United Brethren brought to the new church. To this day, its staff occupies the Administrative Office Building of the former Evangelical United Brethren Church in Dayton, Ohio.

The seventeen committees worked diligently at their tasks and presented the results of their labors to the Joint Commission. Their work was examined by the commissioners and sent on to Dr. Curtis Chambers who served as editor-in-chief. The Plan of Union was published on April 1, 1966, and promptly mailed to the delegates to the Chicago Conferences.

It would be impossible, and probably unnecessary, to tell of negotiations that went on in the seventeen committees. Their work, as amended by the Uniting Conference, is recorded in Part IV of the 1968 *Book of Discipline*. Let us look closely at just one item.

The Methodist *Discipline* of 1964 records the aim of the Board of Missions:

The supreme aim of missions is to make the Lord Jesus Christ known to all persons in all lands as their divine Saviour, to persuade them to become his disciples, and to gather these disciples in Christian churches; to enlist them in the building of the kingdom of God; to co-operate with these churches; to promote world Christian fellowship; and to bring to bear upon all human life the spirit and principles of Christ.[11]

The Evangelical United Brethren *Discipline* of 1967 records the aim of its Board of Missions:

The Gospel is designed for all nations, its field of operation is the whole world, and the church is under solemn obligation to make known its saving truth and power among the peoples of the earth. To this great work we are impelled and encouraged by the command of the Lord and the promises and prophecies of the Holy Scriptures.[12]

The aim of mission set before The United Methodist Church in 1968, because of the labors of the subcommittee dealing with the Board of Missions, was this:

God, Creator, Redeemer, and Life-Giver summons the church to mission in the world. The aims of this mission are:
(1) To witness in all the world, by word and deed, to the self-revelation of God in Jesus Christ and the acts of love by which he reconciles men to himself.
(2) To evoke in men the personal response of repentance and faith through which by God's grace they may find newness of life in righteous, loving relationships with God and their fellowman.
(3) To bring men together into a Christian community for worship and fellowship, and to send men into the world as servants in the struggle for justice and meaning.
(4) To reveal in ministry the love of God for all who suffer.
(5) To move men to live in awareness of the presence and life-giving power of God's Holy Spirit, in acknowledgment of his rule over earthly history, and in confident expectation of the ultimate consummation of his purpose.[13]

Similar exhibits could be made of the statements of purpose of other agencies of the church. What is an aim? Is it not an attempt to say how an agency is going to put its believing into behavior in the here and now? There was an abundance of newness written into the language of *The Book of Discipline*. The doing of what we have written is the difficult way to go.

Enabling Legislation

A project as complicated as this union turned out to be called for a well-marked road map, and that is exactly what the Enabling Legislation came to be. It was a map that grew with the emergence of necessities, but one thing it exhibited above all was that the commissioners intended The United Methodist Church to be a fair-minded church, an inclusive church, and a world church. The Joint Commission worked over the Enabling Legislation right up to the last available hour. It was published August 1, 1966.

Informing the Constituencies

A pamphlet of six chapters entitled *Our Churches Face Union* was published and widely distributed. It included the following chapters:

I—"The History of the Uniting Churches," written by Bishops Paul Garber and Paul Milhouse,

II—"The Faith of the Uniting Churches," written by Bishop Roy Hunter Short,

III—"The Uniting Churches in Action," written by Bishops W. Vernon Middleton and J. Gordan Howard,

IV—"The Structure of the United Church," written by Dr. Paul Washburn,

V—"The Questions and Answers about Union," written by Bishops Howard and Short, and

VI—"The Call to a United Church," written by Bishop Lloyd C. Wicke.

Television, Radio, and Film Commission of The United Methodist Church produced a filmstrip entitled "One Heritage! One Faith! One Church?" which was widely used.

The office of the Evangelical United Brethren Commission published *Interpretations* in twenty-five issues. *Interpretations* set forth decisions that were made by the Joint Commission between November 1, 1965, and October 15, 1966. The publication was mailed to all ministers in the Evangelical United Brethren Church and to commissioners and bishops in both churches. It was, as its name implied, an interpretative piece and did not attempt to sell union.

Church periodicals expressed genuine interest in the union process. Their editors were frequent observers of the commissioners at work. Their pages were open to articles in which the pros and cons of union could be expressed and to articles in which some commissioners could answer questions pertaining to the union. For instance, in September of 1966 *Together* published an article under the title "Two Leaders Answer Questions on The Methodist-Evangelical United Brethren Union." In that article Charles C. Parlin and Paul A. Washburn each answered twelve elementary questions.

Just before the 1966 General Conferences in Chicago, Dr. Curtis Chambers writing in *Central Christian Advocate* said:

In a sense, church union is already taking place in many parts of the country. Yoked fields, where a minister of either denomination serves two congregations, one Methodist and the other Evangelical United Brethren, exist in scores of communities. Many local churches have had joint sessions of their men's or women's organizations. In annual conferences, boards have often extended advisory relationships to members of similar boards in the other denomination. In situations such as these, sentiment for union often runs strong. There are, in fact, some advocates of this technique for church union: first work together at the local level, then come together at the conference and denominational levels.

Dr. Chambers concluded his article with the question that was in the minds of many persons prior to the Chicago General Conferences: "As Methodists and Evangelical United Brethren look at urgent concern from the vantage point of a common historical heritage, they must answer yet another question: Can we best fulfill our mission under God together—or apart?"[14]

7

Contention over Union

One would think that a proposal for a new church affecting the lives of 11 million Christians would have caused more contention in the churches than was the case in this instance. A suggestion box was created in the office of the Evangelical United Brethren Commission on Union, but it was not used by many persons or groups. Some contention came from individuals at the grass roots of the churches, some from professional theologians and schools of theology, some from bishops, and some appeared in *The Christian Century* and in the journals of the two churches. In this chapter these forms of contention will be illustrated.

Contention at the Grass Roots

Individuals exhibited both anxiety and affirmation about the union.

An Evangelical United Brethren pastor in Arizona expressed apprehension about the union in a letter dated May 11, 1965. He had seven concerns: (1) Will the Evangelical United Brethren Church entirely lose its identity? (2) Will the new church through its ministry and membership maintain allegiance to the plan of salvation based on biblical grounds? (3) Will the union be negotiated by a few without consideration for the wishes of the majority? (4) Will there be so much compromise as to jeopardize the achievement of a higher morality? (5) What will happen to church members who choose to be Evangelical United Brethren rather than Methodists? (6) Can greater size be equated with quality? and (7) Does not the Evangelical United Brethren Church have a greater future as a separate and distinct denomination?

A Methodist from Iowa suggested that the whole idea of union should be subjected to one of two parliamentary procedures. He said it should either "be postponed indefinitely" or "laid on the table." He claimed much support for such actions for the following reasons: (1) The present Plan of Union is out of step with the churches of the world in their quest for unity. (2) Apart from fundamental spiritual renewal, our labors for union are in vain. (3) Racial segregation is a stigma with which the plan does not deal forthrightly. (4) The plan does not propose a new creed that speaks meaningfully to men of today. (5) Academic requirements for ministers are at variance. *{It must be noted that a study made by the Division of Higher Education and Ministry of the Methodist Church reveals that the percentage of ministers with complete college and theological school educations in the two churches stood just a little over 60 percent, with Evangelical United Brethren ministers holding a slightly higher percentage.}* (6) Ministerial pension problems are too great. (7) Minimum wage requirements will make for larger demands upon Annual Conference budgets. (8) No provision has been made for union of structures. (9) This union is no union, but a genial swallowing of the smaller church by the larger. (10) Time is not of the essence in this matter. Only renewal matters.

The Reverend Cecil R. Findley of Kansas, a member of the Evangelical United Brethren Commission, was given to writing poetry about the union. One of his finest was written on September 10, 1965. It expressed the mood of most of the commissioners on both sides.

> **Hymn of Renewal**
> Renew thy church, O God,
> Empower us from above
> To brother all the sons of men
> And lift them to thy love.
>
> Renew thy church, O God,
> With gladness and with grace;
> Let us in lowly servanthood
> Reveal the Master's face.
>
> Renew thy church, O God,
> Give us the Christlike soul
> To dream, to dare, to die for thee,
> To reach thy kingdom's goal.
>
> Renew thy church, O God,
> In all its ancient power;
> Arm us as messengers of Christ.
> Make this our finest hour.
>
> Renew thy church, O God,
> The hour is growing late.
> The time is coming for thee to rule
> And love to conquer hate.[1]

The Evangelical United Brethren pastor from Arizona and the Methodist pastor from Iowa expressed typical apprehensions about the union, but Mr. Findley expressed hope both for the success of the union effort and for the renewal of the church.

Contention from Theologians

Professors and students at Evangelical Theological Seminary in Naperville, Illinois; United Theological Seminary in Dayton, Ohio; and Methodist Theological School in Delaware, Ohio, sincerely and earnestly tried to impact the plan of union. The Naperville group called themselves Evangelical United Brethren for Church Renewal and quickly picked up support from several Methodists. They forwarded to the Joint Commissions a well-written document entitled "Issues for A Union: A Biblical and Theological Perspective." In the document, proposals for the Plan of Union were based upon the conviction that "biblical and theological issues are basic to our union." Four issues were discussed.

The first issue was racial inclusiveness. The paper said, "In the Church there is to be no distinction between Jew and Greek, slave or free, all are one in Christ Jesus. This Biblical faith must shape the goals and purposes of the Church. Therefore, trying to decide the issue of the Central Jurisdiction only as an administrative problem is to miss the basic theological issue at stake. We would affirm that the continuation of the Central Jurisdiction is an institutional betrayal of the nature of the Church." Later in the discussion of this issue, the writers concluded, "We are committed to a new church for a new day . . . a church uniting **both** denominations and races, to the glory of God and the service of the world in the name of Jesus Christ."

The second issue concerned ecumenical commitment. Using illustrations of how the Evangelical United Brethren Church had entered the United Church of Christ in the Philippines and how the Methodist Church had not, and of how similar positions were taken by the two denominations with respect to the United Campus Christian fellowship, the paper went on to say, "We heartily support confessional unions, like that between the Methodist and Evangelical United Brethren Churches. But we do not support such a confessional union if it diminishes, and it need not, our capacity or freedom to achieve unity of 'all in each place.' "

Third among the issues was the issue of polity. Under this theme, the paper discussed the episcopacy and superintendency. With regard to episcopacy, the paper stated, "Should bishops be elected for life, as are Methodist bishops, or re-elected every four years, as are Evangelical United Brethren bishops? Much depends on the functions our bishops are to fulfill. Our theological commitment and democratic procedure would indicate that if bishops in the new church are to continue to be primarily administrative they should stand for re-election. If, however, we should decide that we need bishops whose major function is pastoral and spiritual leadership that keeps the church united and true to its Biblical and historical mission, then electing them for life, would follow."

The difference between district superintendents serving as extensions of the bishops' office and conference superintendents serving as officers of the

Annual Conference and amenable to the Annual Conference was raised as another polity issue. The paper observed that district superintendents were part of an authoritarian system and that conference superintendents were part of a more presbyterial system. This issue was summarized in this sentence, "Finally, as we look toward greater unity with other confessions, a pattern of more pastoral and apostolic bishops with elected administrators would move us somewhat away from our more authoritarian patterns and closer to the polity of our brethren in the Episcopal, Presybterian and more congregational denominations."

Fourth among the issues was that of mission and membership in the local congregation. Under this theme, several profound insights were emphasized, insights with which no Christian who cares about the future of the church could take issue. A few sentences will suffice as illustrations: "The major problem facing Christ's people today is the loss of their own sense of identity and purpose in the world. . . . We would affirm that standards of membership and patterns of action can not be decided except as one defines the Biblical nature of the church and its mission. We believe the Christian church is called by God to be the vanguard of the new humanity he is seeking to create [I Peter 2:9-10]. . . . The church does not **have** a mission, it **is** mission. . . . We urge that the new *Discipline* lead us together into precisely that—discipline, disciplined life together and disciplined mission."

The conclusion of the paper includes the following paragraph:

But beyond this, we are committed to hearing Christ's call for a new church, one open to its mission in a changing world, one willing itself to change anything save its loyalty and faith in Jesus Christ. The Christian is always being called to die. Both our denominations must be willing to die that something new might be born. But it must be so that new life may be born, not aging institutions perpetuated. Nor are we willing to die for anything less than our deepest commitments to Jesus Christ, commitments expressed in our Biblical and theological convictions.[2]

Evangelical United Brethren for Church Renewal tried to gain support for their proposals by sending an article written by Professor James E. Will to *The Christian Century*. The article carried the title "Union without Renewal" and appeared in May of 1965. It emphasized the same issues as those discussed above. A reply written by the Reverend Paul Washburn entitled "Is this Renewal?" appeared in the same magazine in June of 1965.

Professors of Methodist Theological School in Ohio joined with professors of United Theological Seminary in the preparation of two papers which were sent to the Joint Commission. The first paper urged the abandonment of the jurisdictional system, especially of the Central Jurisdiction. It said, "We express our loyal opposition to the Plan of Union because we are convinced that the jurisdictional system perpetuates our brokenness and denies our true unity. . . Another aspect of the jurisdictional system which is objectionable is the fact that it came into existence in 1939 in order to establish segregation in The Methodist Church and has been perpetuated ever since for that same sinful purpose. . . . This demands a constitution which not only eliminates the Central Jurisdiction but which also either eliminates the jurisdictional system or so circumscribes its powers that it is no longer an effective instrument of racism."

The other paper prepared by the same group was entitled "The Ecumenical Issue in Church Union." Seeking to help from the ecumenical stance of the proposed church, the paper said, "As the new church's ecumenical stance is shaped, care must be taken that: (1) this union be viewed as a step toward the ever-growing realization of the unity of all Christians, (2) this union be viewed as a unique opportunity to demonstrate what the demands of unity are for denominations seeking to perform God's will in our time."

These proposals also appeared in *The Christian Century* in an article prepared by Professor Paul M. Minus of the Methodist Theological School in Ohio and Professor Arthur C. Core of United Theological Seminary. Appearing in February, 1966, the article was entitled "The United Methodist Church—Critique and Proposal."

The two schools of theology in Ohio offered jointly a seminar in church history taught by Professors Core and DeWire of the Dayton seminary and Professor Minus of the Delaware seminary. Two questionnaires were sent to lay and clergypersons in Ohio—66 percent of Evangelical United Brethren and 54 percent of Methodists responded. Since this course and this questioning were conducted in early 1966, some of the findings are particularly interesting. Among these findings are the following: "(1) among the laity there is good correlation between the feelings of general Christian unity and the Evangelical United Brethren-Methodist union; (2) limited as this survey is, we must conclude that **theology had no part** in determining a person's position on the union; (3) given that of persons surveyed 15% were against union, 25% were 'on the fence' and 60% were for union we can conclude that the 'fence sitters' hold the key to the success or failure of the union."

Thinking and committed Christians find in these proposals from professors and students of theology compelling and constraining issues. The Joint Commission on Church Union was impacted by these issues as can be demonstrated by the final formulation of the Constitution and the Enabling Legislation. To claim, however, that The United Methodist Church is perfect with regard to racism, ecumenicity, polity, or discipline would overstate the case. These issues are still before us as the unfinished business of an unfinished church sixteen years after union.

Contention Among Bishops

Bishops from the Methodist Church were seriously disadvantaged in understanding the Plan of Union when compared to bishops of the

Evangelical United Brethren Church. Only a few Methodist bishops served on the Joint Commission while all seven Evangelical United Brethren bishops were members. Between November of 1963 and March of 1966, no less than eleven major papers on the union were prepared by Bishops Fred Pierce Corson, Costen J. Harrell, F. Gerald Ensley, J. Gordan Howard, Kenneth W. Copeland, Roy H. Short, Reuben H. Mueller, W. Ralph Ward, Jr., Eugene Frank, and James K. Mathews and presented to the Council of Bishops of the Methodist Church.

A paper by retired Bishop Costen J. Harrell reveals interest in: (1) questions on ministerial orders, (2) questions regarding appointment of district superintendents, (3) questions about the Articles of Religion, (4) questions about a called session of the General Conference, (5) questions about the consecration of bishops, (6) questions about quarterly and church conferences, and (7) sundry questions about the proposed name for the new church, the twelve-year period of transition, and the Program Council.

Many other questions were raised by bishops of the Methodist Church, but Bishops Wicke, Short, and Ensley tried to answer those questions.

Bishop W. Kenneth Copeland addressed the Council of Bishops in Louisville, Kentucky, on April 14, 1966. He said in his address, "I am in favor of the union of The Evangelical United Brethren Church and The Methodist Church. I believe it to be a **union** and not a merger, that a new denomination can well be a renewed segment of Christ's kingdom." Deeper into his address, Bishop Copeland said, "I believe there are great devotions that draw us together. We share a common devotion to the three basic symbols of ecclesiastical union namely, our minstry, our membership and the Sacraments. We are drawn together in a common devotion to the evangelistic and social task. Finally, we are drawn together by a common devotion to the essential oneness of the Body of Christ. We believe we are already one in His Love—we must be one in our witness to His Love. We are called to make valid and vital our commitment to One Lord, One Body, One Faith, One Witness, One World."[3]

Bishop Copeland's address carried special weight because he had come out of the Methodist Protestant Church in 1939 and had found the union of 1939 valid and effective.

On March 9, 1966, the Commission on Ecumenical Affairs of the Methodist Church adopted a resolution on the union that had been prepared by Bishop James K. Mathews. The resolution says in part, "What is proposed is not just a merger for convenience, after the manner of the market-place, but a living union within the body of Christ. Together we shall be able to walk more closely along the pilgrim way. Our summons is to a new seriousness in ecumenical involvement and to fuller accord with the prayer of Our Lord that his disciples might be one. . . . God, we believe, affords to this generation an exhilarating experience of fuller unity which he gave to another generation in 1939. Let us avail ourselves of this, not for comfort but for conscience's sake. We are under no compulsion but the compulsion of love and the obligation and joy of responding to God's action among us."[4]

The deportment of bishops in the uniting churches reveals that they understood themselves to be responsible for oversight of both the temporal and spiritual concerns of the churches. They were not just administrators. They were also shepherds of the flock of Christ.

Contention in the Church Press

Church publications assisted greatly with dissemination of information about the union. A fair indication of this fact was the publication of two articles in the Methodist *Together* in June of 1966. Under the title "Methodist-Evangelical United Brethren Union Now or Later," Bishop Lance Webb authored the "Now" portion and the Reverend Richard Cain authored the "Later" portion.

Bishop Webb, in support of his "union now" position, said he was for union now because he believed that faithful, persistent following-through on the present plan could and would call forth the necessary grass-roots discussions essential to union. He held to his position because he believed that the only way renewal could come to the church was through the confrontation of each other in worship, in fellowship, and in agonizing discussion. He believed that the only way to find an adequate structure was in going forward with the present plan, and he believed that union was not only a practical but a Christian necessity.

Dr. Richard Cain wrote in support of his "union later" position that the work of the Joint Commission had been done by too few people and by a group of limited representation. He said that the areas of his concern had to do with the absence of a new doctrinal standards statement, with the continuance of racial segregation in the church, with the twelve-year rule, with the name for the new church, and with the absence of a new social creed. He concluded his article with the following words:

Let me repeat that my opposition to this plan is not opposition to the idea of uniting The Methodist and Evangelical United Brethren Churches. They should be together. But their union should solve problems, not postpone them. It should further the ecumenical involvement and contributions of each, not seriously impair the ability of the united church to move vigorously in further union discussions. It should be the sort of plan that commands enthusiastic support by huge majorities of both churches, not one that inculcates apathy and indifference due to lack of involvement.[5]

Church and Home of the Evangelical United Brethren Church and *The Christian Advocate* and *Together* of the Methodist Church worked diligently to keep the proposed union before the people of the two churches. They published editorials and articles too numerous to list and whole series of articles that dealt courteously and frankly with the concerns of members.

Why was there contention in, and between, the churches over union? Some of it could be attributed to individual minds with narrow horizons of churchmanship. Some of it could be attributed to the desires of nonparticipating persons to participate. Most of it could be attributed to the love the members of the churches held for their traditional denominations. One fact is clear. The contention was essential to the ongoing process of preparation of the Plan of Union.

8

The Chicago General Conferences—1966

Chicago's Conrad Hilton Hotel was the physical setting for four days of simultaneous sessions of the General Conferences of the Evangelical United Brethren Church and the Methodist Church. The Methodist General Conference had been officially designated as an adjourned session of that church's General Conference of 1964. Three items were on its limited agenda: the proposed union, a progress report on the denomination's intention to eliminate the racially segregated Central Jurisdiction from the structures of the church, and the dedication of the new Methodist *Book of Hymns*.

The Evangelical United Brethren General Conference was that church's regular quadrennial conference. While the conference spent the first four days, from November 8 to 11, with attention focused on the Plan of Union, it had many other items on its agenda. This conference finally adjourned on November 17.

The International Ballroom housed the Methodist Conference, and the Grand Ballroom housed the Evangelical United Brethren Conference. A corridor twenty feet wide separated the two conferences. Many conversations between delegates to the two conferences took place in that narrow hallway. One organization comprised of members from both churches known as the Church Renewal Caucus seemed to headquarter in this strategic place and had a significant effect upon both conferences.

Bishop Frederick B. Newell presented the homily for the Methodist communion service. During the homily, he said:

I think I have detected in the corridors of the church, as men have approached this union, apprehension, fear and criticism. It is time now to lay aside the heaviness that has so easily beset us and to approach this ecumenical state with faith, courage and confidence.

Draw near with faith that the new church will be the Church in Renewal; that it will not be a church beset with bickering, apathy or indecision, but a new church challenging the evils of this world.

A church that will never relax its determination to rid the nations of the evils of the malignancy of poverty. A church that will not be at peace with racism either within or without its borders, no matter what ethnic group is involved. A church that seeing its Lord standing on the shore of Galilee before the multitudes and having compassion on them will not be at rest while hunger stalks the earth.

A church that will not be afraid of the ghetto nor compromised by the suburb. A church that will not be conformed to the slaughter of innocent people. A church that will never be silent in the face of any issue threatening the welfare of mankind. A church that will not be confined by any boundary nor restricted by any peril.

Draw near with faith that the new church will be the church of revelation. We approach this ecumenical step in the age of great denial—and in such an hour in history I say to you the new church must be the church of revelation—a revealing Church.

Draw near with faith that the new church will be the church of redemptive power. A church that will never deviate from its belief that mankind can be transformed. A church that will not silence its proclamation of the redemptive power of a living Lord.[1]

Bishop Roy H. Short delivered the Episcopal Message in behalf of the Methodist Council of Bishops on Tuesday morning, November 8. In it he said:

What is immediately before us as we assemble here is essentially a single decision—the decision as to whether we shall take for Methodism at this General Conference the first constitutional step toward uniting The Methodist Church and The Evangelical United Brethren Church.

As we now come as a church to a momentous time of decision, we find ourselves living first of all with decisions taken by our fathers in both churches a century and a half ago, and by subsequent generations in both bodies across the intervening years. . . . It is no mere accident of ecclesiastical history that The Methodist Church and the Evangelical United Brethren Church should at this relatively late hour be considering the possibility of union. The two churches in their beginning days in the United States were largely affected by the same evangelical revival. The general faith which they professed; the practices of personal piety which they inculcated; the strong emphasis which was theirs upon evangelism and conversion, and upon Christian growth and faithfulness in good works; and even the broad forms of church government followed, were all essentially alike. The leaders of both churches were intimate friends and willing co-laborers.

If union between The Methodist Church and The Evangelical United Brethren Church can conceivably put us as churches into position to puruse our mission more effectively in this our day and in the tomorrows immediately ahead, then certainly it merits our serious consideration.

Finally, if union between The Methodist Church and the Evangelical United Brethren Church can offer fresh hope that the church as we envisage it in union, and as we may be able to build it together in the years immediately ahead, shall be truly evangelical; then such a union is indeed a union in which the entire Christian world has a stake. Strong advocates are not wanting at the moment for the viewpoint that the church in our day must be "truly reformed." It is for those who stand in the tradition in which Methodists and Evangelical United Brethren stand to insist that it shall also be "truly evangelical," preaching a positive gospel of redeeming love; expecting to witness the twin miracles of conversion and Christian growth in the lives of those who respond in faith; daring to believe that all the kingdoms of this world can become the kingdoms of our Lord and of His Christ; and with eyes and heart forever turned outward toward all the lost and broken and despairing and mistreated and disinherited of earth.

Above all others, our Lord Himself is involved in what we may do here. The church is not our church but His church. . . . It is ours in this moment of decision to try to hear what God may be speaking to us as a church today; and when we have heard, to dare to obey with faith, with courage and with the assurance that He who has begun a good work in us as a people will Himself finally bring it to completion.[2]

Across that narrow corridor in the Evangelical United Brethren General Conference, Bishop J. Gordon Howard read the Episcopal Message in behalf of the Board of Bishops. After speaking three short paragraphs about the Consultation on Church Union, he spoke four short paragraphs about the proposed union. Could it have been that Evangelical United Brethren people needed less persuasion than the Methodist people did? Or could the brevity of the statement seem only supplementary to a previous statement of the Board of Bishops declaring support of the union? The four paragraphs follow:

Since 1946 when The Evangelical United Brethren Church was formed, we have been concerned with the possibility of further unions. In the 1946 uniting conference and the subsequent four General Conferences, declarations have been made authorizing study and effort looking toward possible unions. For twelve years before 1962 the Commission on Church Union held probing conversations and exchanged correspondence with several denominations. Such efforts were met with friendliness, but only The Methodist Church indicated immediate interest. The 1962 General Conference instructed the Commission on Church Union to negotiate seriously with the Methodists and, if possible, bring to this 1966 General Conference a plan of union for consideration.

The Commission on Church Union has been true to its assignment. Months of time and efforts by scores of persons have been spent during the quadrennium to prepare a Plan of Union and a *Discipline* for a proposed new church. These documents have been circulated and studied. They have been in your hands as delegates to this General Conference. The time has come for decision.

The decision on union with The Methodist Church will be the supreme issue of this General Conference. Whatever action is taken, affirmative or negative, will affect our church forever. If ever there was a time for prayer, wisdom and courage, the time is now. Ten days hence will be too late. Seldom do men and women at a given moment consciously confront a decision which has such ramifications not only for themselves, but for their children's children in the unending years ahead. This is the time earnestly to pray for a portion of the "depth of the riches and wisdom and knowledge of God."

The mind of the Board of Bishops regarding the action of this General Conference concerning church union was set forth in a declaration printed in *Church and Home Magazine* and circulated in annual conference sessions last spring and summer. The bishops hope and pray the decision, whatever it is, will be made for the right reasons.

It would be tragic if any vote would be cast for reasons petty and parochial. Voting should be prayerful, seeking the will of God. Voting should be unselfish and the result of long-range, broad gauge thinking in terms of ultimates. Voting should consider the welfare of our descendants who will carry the burdens of the future.[3]

The brief portions of much longer messages from Bishops Newell, Short, and Howard, spoken in behalf of the Council of Bishops and the Board of Bishops, revealed affirmative and aggressive leadership in the matter of union from the bishops of both churches. All seven bishops of the Evangelical United Brethren Church had served faithfully on the Joint Commission, and while only five members of the Council of Bishops of the Methodist Church had served on that commission, the Methodist bishops, as indicated earlier, had done their homework on the Plan of Union.

Four parts comprised the Plan of Union as it was presented to the conferences: I—The Constitution, II—Doctrinal Statements and the General Rules, III—Social Principles, and IV—Organization and Administration. In addition, two supplemental reports and the Enabling Legislation (the plan for effecting the union) were presented, but the conferences were asked to focus their energies on Part I and the Enabling Legislation because these portions of the plan would substantially affect the Constitution called up for vote on Friday, November 11.

Bishop Lloyd C. Wicke of New York, chairman of the Methodist Commission on Union, presented highlights of the Plan of Union to the Methodist Conference, describing the pending decision as "a holy gamble." After his presentation the conference voted to refer the documents to the standing legislative committees for their consideration and for reports back to the conference.

The Reverend Paul Washburn, executive director of the Evangelical United Brethren Commission, presented the union documents to the Evangelical United Brethren Conference with exhortations:

Surely, we will make our pilgrim way through the next hours with confidence: (1) in God, (2) in one another, (3) in what goes on between us, (4) in the decision we will make. . . . Joy will be our companion and the companion of our confidence, for here we intend to do that which is supremely right for two churches.

After the presentation, the plan was referred to twenty discussion groups.

It was the understanding of both conferences that: (1) an Order of the Day be set for Friday, November 11, for a vote on Part I, the Constitution and the Enabling Legislation, (2) that the Constitution and the Enabling Legislation could not be amended unilaterally by either General Conference, (3) that proposed amendments rising in either conference shall be referred to the Joint Conference Committee, and (4) any proposal referred to the Joint Conference Committee shall be considered there and referred back to the two General Conferences as promptly as possible. If the proposal gained approval in the Joint Conference Committee and majority affirmative votes in both General Conferences, the proposal would become an amendment to the Plan of Union.

It was the plan that the Joint Conference Committee would serve in a way comparable to the ways of Joint Conference Committees in the United States Congress that attempt to reconcile legislation pending in the Senate and the House of Representatives, bringing its conclusions back to the respective bodies for action.

Pressure was exerted in both conferences to enlarge the Joint Conference Committee. Proponents of enlargement observed that the committee lacked representation from pastors of local churches and laypersons who were not denominationally employed. Three persons were added to the committee by each church, and the committee's membership finally included the following persons:

Methodists	Evangelical United Brethren
Bishop Lloyd C. Wicke	Bishop Reuben H. Mueller
Bishop F. Gerald Ensley	Bishop Harold R. Heininger
Bishop Roy H. Short	Bishop J. Gordon Howard
Dr. Charles C. Parlin	Bishop Hermann W. Kaebnick
Dr. J. Otis Young	Dr. Paul Washburn
Dr. J. Wesley Hole	Dr. Curtis A. Chambers
Dr. Norman L. Trott	Dr. L. L. Huffman
Mr. Lovick Pierce	Mr. Torrey A. Kaatz
Dr. Emory Bucke	Dr. Charles E. Kachel
Miss Theressa Hoover	Mr. J. Britain Winter
Dr. Finis Crutchfield	Mrs. D. Dwight Grove
Dr. Nat G. Long	Dr. Harvey C. Hahn
Mr. James Walker	Mr. Rolland Osborne

It is revealing to note that of the members of this committee eight were from the Northeastern Jurisdiction, nine were from the North Central, four were from the Southeastern, three were from the South Central, and two were from the Western, but not one was from the Central Jurisdiction. Only two women and one president of a School of Theology served on the committee.

Amendments to the Constitution

Seven amendments to the Plan of Union were proposed by the Evangelical United Brethren Conference. Four of the seven resulted in amendments to the Constitution.

First among the four was addition to the Preamble to the Constitution of the following paragraphs:

The church is a community of all true believers under the Lordship of Christ. It is the redeemed and redeeming fellowship in which the Word of God is preached by men divinely called, and the Sacraments are duly administered according to Christ's own appointment. Under the discipline of the Holy Spirit the church seeks to provide for the maintenance of worship, the edification of believers and the redemption of the world.

The Church of Jesus Christ exists in and for the world and its very dividedness is a hindrance to its mission in the world.

The second amendment dropped a sentence from Article II. The dropped sentence read: "In other than legal documents (the name) The Methodist Church may be used."

The third amendment dropped one phrase from Article IX, namely "appointed by the bishop." This phrase had not previously been in the Methodist Constitution, but provision for bishops to appoint district superintendents was to remain in Part IV, paragraph 335.

The fourth amendment added the conference president of United Methodist Men to the membership of Annual Conferences.

Eight amendments to the Constitution were proposed by the Methodist Conference. Seven of them prevailed, but one of the major debates of the conferences revolved around the one proposal which failed to gain approval.

One proposal amended the Constitution in order to grant to a General Conference the right to expand its agenda by a two-thirds vote.

A second proposal amended the paragraph dealing with hymnals and rituals by removing the letter *s* from the word *hymnals* and the word *rituals*. The agreement was that in The United Methodist Church the continued use of the hymnals and the rituals currently in use in the two churches would be valid. It seemed probable, however, that new hymnals and new rituals would one day appear. One fact that escaped the notice of almost everyone was that *The Book of Ritual* of the Evangelical United Brethren Church included a ritual for the Dedication of Infants. Thus, The United Methodist Church had approved, unwittingly, a service for the Dedication of Infants.

A third proposed amendment came from German delegations to the conference and clearly gave to Central Conferences power to adapt the general *Disciplines* of the church to local requirements.

A fourth amendment authorized Central Conferences to create a judicial body to pass upon administrative questions arising under a revised and adapted *Discipline* of a Central Conference.

A fifth amendment left the matter of definition of ministers open so that ensuing General Conferences would be free to amend those definitions. It also left open the issue of the definition of the status of a deacon and whether there should be one or two orders.

A sixth amendment provided, "The bishops of the several Jurisdictional and Central Conferences shall preside in the sessions of their respective Conferences." This proposal was brought forward by the German delegation.

A seventh amendment was designed to facilitate, strengthen, encourage, and hasten the elimination of any racial structures in the proposed church. It proposed the inclusion in the Enabling Legislation of a resolution passed in the Methodist Conference to do everything within its power to eliminate the Central Jurisdiction and also the merger of the separate black Annual Conferences with the conferences of the Regional Jurisdictions. All members of the Joint Conference Committee and both General Conferences enthusiastically approved this amendment to the Enabling Legislation. From the beginning of negotiations, no member of the Evangelical United Brethren Commission on Union was in favor of allowing the Central Jurisdiction to be a part of the structure of the new church.

Bishop Roy Short commenting in early 1967 upon the Methdist General Conference of 1966 said: "Beyond doubt the overshadowing concern of the General Conference was that the right thing should be done with reference to race." Seeking to quiet the accusation that union with the Evangelical United Brethren Church tends to bypass the obligation of the church to abolish segregation, Bishop Short made five important observations:

1. Evangelical United Brethren union does away immediately with the embarrassment of provision in the Constitution for a jurisdiction based upon race.
2. The union provides that no unit of the church shall be so structured as to exclude anyone on the basis of race.
3. The plan for union provides definitely that immediately no episcopal area can be composed exclusively of black conferences.
4. Evangelical United Brethren union provides for an integrated episcopacy throughout the church, with every college of bishops having within it some bishops elected by The Evangelical United Brethren Church, some elected by the Central Jurisdiction and some elected by the other jurisdictions.
5. Amendment seven discussed above provides definitely that the spirit and intent of the report of the Committee on Inter-jurisdictional Relations shall be applied also to the union.

It is fair to assume that the union of the two churches hastened the demise of the Central Jurisdiction and mandated racial equality in The United Methodist Church.

Article V (Ecumenical Relations) proved to be the issue over which the longest debate raged. The Plan of Union proposed the following text:

As a part of the Church Universal, The United Methodist Church believes that the Lord of the Church is calling Christians everywhere to strive toward unity and therefore it will seek, and work for, unity at all levels of church life; through world relations with other Methodist churches and united churches related to The Methodist Church or The Evangelical United Brethren Church; through councils of churches; and through plans of union with churches of Methodist or other denomination traditions.[4]

Dr. Albert C. Outler had drafted the proposed amendment and the Church Renewal Caucus supported it and lobbied enthusiastically for it. The proposed text reads:

As part of the church universal, The United Methodist Church believes that Christ calls all Christians to receive and manifest his gift of unity in faith in order to have a more effective mission and service of his church. It will, therefore, seek and work for larger unity in faith and order at all levels of church life in responsible consultation and negotiation with all other interested churches, both Methodist and others.[5]

The Evangelical United Brethren members of the Joint Conference Committee felt that the proposed amendment in two respects fell short of the ecumenical stance they hoped for in the new church: first, the new church should continue its active participation in councils of churches and in the Consultation on Church Union; and, second, they thought it essential to mention a continuing relationship with united churches around the world related to the Evangelical United Brethren Church. Earlier, during the formation of the Plan of Union, the Church Renewal Group had been very critical of the ecumenical cooperation of the Methodist Church citing how, in the Philippines, the Evangelical United Brethren Church went into the United Church of the Philippines and the Methodist Philippine Church did not. Evangelical United Brethren delegates wanted assurance that The United Methodist Church would continue allegiance to, and support of, the united churches. Because Methodists on the Joint Conference Committee met staunch resistance from Evangelical United Brethren members of the committee, the proposal to amend Article V died in committee.

When all the negotiating was ended, there was a brief flurry of speeches, both pro and con, in both conferences. The process was interrupted at 11:00 A.M. to remember the armistice and what World War II had cost, for it was November 11. An agreement had been reached that the results of the voting would be kept secret until both votes had been taken. It was evident that the Methodists had concluded their voting, because the Evangelical United Brethren Conference was surrounded by Methodist spectators long before the vote was taken. Mr. J. Britain Winter submitted the same resolution to the Evangelical United Brethren Conference that had been submitted to the Methodist Conference:

Resolved, that the Constitution of the United Methodist Church as amended be and the same is hereby approved and adopted. Resolved further, that the Enabling Legislation for the formation of The United Methodist Church as amended be and the same is hereby approved and adopted.[6]

The vote in the Evangelical Brethren Conference was 325 in favor of union and 88 against, or 78.6 percent, just 3.6 percent more than the required 75 percent majority. The vote in the Methodist Conference was 749 in favor and 40 opposed, or 94.9 percent, with only a two-thirds majority required for passage. By these victories in both conferences, the Constitution of The United Methodist Church and the Enabling Legislation to form The United Methodist Church were remanded to all of the Annual Conferences in the two churches for their vote.

A gracious act is hidden in the Proceedings of the Evangelical United Brethren Conference. It was a statement made by Bishop J. Gordon Howard just prior to the vote on union. The item reads as follows: "Bishop Howard, the presiding bishop, suggested that after the vote is taken there should be no public demonstration. Whatever the outcome of the vote, there will be some hearts glad and some sad. Each group should respect the convictions of the other."

Joint Session

Bishop Richard C. Raines, president of the Council of Bishops of the Methodist Church, extended an invitation to the Evangelical United Brethren Conference to meet at 2:00 P.M. with the Methodist Conference for a brief period of devotion. The invitation was gladly accepted. During that period of devotion, Bishop Fred Pierce Corson called it "an historic moment when we meet as one." Bishop Frederick B. Newell made a statement about the action of the Methodist Conference. Bishop Reuben H. Mueller introduced the bishops of the Evangelical United Brethren Church. He said during brief remarks that:

As I have been sitting here turning these things over in my mind, I thought to myself—I wonder what Francis Asbury is saying to his dear German friend Philip William Otterbein; and how Jacob Albright has finally resolved his differences with Francis Asbury about the German language? And how they have to say to each other in the courts of heaven, as they are in the cloud of witnesses that surround us, "At last our children have started back home together."

Please, God, this shall be not only the first step but that the necessary steps in our annual conferences will be taken in the same spirit and spiritual devotion and dedication as this big major step has been taken.[7]

Bishop Raines spoke last, saying:

The delegates came here convinced that we Methodists ought to join the ecumenical journey in earnest and that the first step was union with our Evangelical United Brethren friends. Very quickly the morale and the will of the conference emerged.

It may be that the record seen in historical perspective will show that no General Conference of The Methodist Church moved so far or so fast in so short a time towards setting a new course for our church, a new name, a new church, a new constitution, a new flexibility, a new readiness to face the future in obedience to God's leading.

The first step is to unite, but the underlying and continuing concern must be for renewal.

But I believe that God has already begun to renew his church. Where the people have sought to discover the New Testament image of the nature and mission of the church and have seen that the church is Christ's and not ours, that it was established to accomplish his purposes and not ours, to change our wills and purposes and not His; renewal has already begun.

Where his people have come to see that the proper concern of Christ's church is not just a so-called religious or spiritual aspect of life but all of life, that God loves the world; renewal has begun.[8]

The joined conferences joined hands and sang "Blest Be the Tie That Binds." Bishop George Edward Epp, the senior bishop of the Evangelical United Brethren Church, spoke the benediction:

And now, may grace, mercy and peace from God the Father, the Son and the Holy Spirit abide with us now and always and let all the people say "Amen."

The Methodist General Conference had finished its work, but the Evangelical United Brethren General Conference continued for six more days. During those six days, the conference took one action of high importance to the process of union. It appointed a Commission on Unity to try to reconcile those who disagreed with the proposed union in the Northwest Canada Conference, the Montana Conference, and the Pacific Northwest Conference.

The two General Conferences of 1966, after much study, debate, and negotiation, had taken first steps toward amending the Constitution of the Methodist Church and the Constitutional Law of the Evangelical United Brethren Church by approving the Constitution of The United Methodist Church. Final adoption of that constitution awaited the affirmative vote of the aggregate number of votes cast in the Annual Conferences of both churches. Thus, the weeks and months between November 11, 1966, and April 23, 1968, were filled with debate and anticipation of the possible union. Factually, union was assured on Tuesday, June 25, 1967, when the Sandusky Conference of the Evangelical United Brethren Church cast the deciding votes.

9

From Chicago 1966 to Dallas 1968

Huge tasks weighed heavily upon the Joint Commission on Union as it made its way from Chicago to Dallas: the reworking and republishing of the Plan of Union including the revisions approved in Chicago; the rewriting of large portions of Part IV—Organization and Administration; the further interpretation of the plan, especially for Annual Conferences; the gradual tallying of the yes and no votes being taken in the Annual Conferences; the attempt of an Evangelical United Brethren Commission on Unity to find reconciliation with dissident majorities of the Montana, Northwest Canada, and Pacific Northwest Conferences; the projection of practical matters such as budgets for the new quadrennium; and the development of an appropriate celebration of the union.

Reworking of Part IV

The Chicago General Conferences had finalized the Constitution and Enabling Legislation and sent them on to the Annual Conferences of both churches for either approval or rejection. In each church, constitutional amendments required a two-thirds aggregate majority of those present and voting in the Annual Conferences. In a way, Part IV—Organization and Administration had been frozen, also, because it had been "adopted in principle" by the Chicago Conferences. It could be amended by a majority vote in the Uniting Conference, unless one-third of the delegates from either church called for a vote by denominations. In that case, an amendment would require a majority vote in both delegations. Interestingly, this provision for voting by delegations was never employed at the Uniting Conference.

By February of 1968, fourteen months after the Chicago Conferences, the Joint Commission had published a report to the Uniting Conference that included thirty-three revisions for Part IV. Included in the revisions were total rewrites of the chapters on "The Local Church," "The Ministry," "The Program Council," and "The Board of the Laity." For the rewriting of the

105

four chapters, largely new committees were appointed, including new personnel and new leadership.

The Local Church

With Bishop W. McFerrin Stowe serving as chairman, Bishop J. Gordon Howard as vice-chairman, and the Reverend Donald App as secretary, the Committee on the Local Church sought to meet the objections raised in Chicago. The committee, however, retained the definition of the local church that had been developed by the earlier committee.

A local church is a community of all true believers under the Lordship of Christ. It is the redemptive fellowship in which the Word of God is preached by men divinely called, and the Sacraments are duly administered according to Christ's own appointment. Under the discipline of the Holy Spirit the church exists for the maintenance of worship, the edification of believers, and the redemption of the world.

The church of Jesus Christ exists in and for the world. It is primarily at the level of the local church that the church encounters the world. The local church is a strategic base from which Christians move out to the structures of society.

The local church is a connectional society of persons who have professed their faith in Christ, have been baptized, have assumed the vows of membership in The United Methodist Church, and are associated in fellowship as a local United Methodist Church, "in order that they may hear the word of God, receive the Sacraments, and carry forward the work which Christ has committed to his Church." Such a society of believers, being within The United Methodist Church and subject to its *Discipline,* is also an inherent part of the Church Universal, which is composed of all who accept Jesus Christ as Lord and Savior, and which we declare in the Apostles' Creed to be the holy catholic Church.[1]

This new chapter on the local church, as developed and submitted to the Uniting Conference, included meanings and methods promising renewal of the local congregations.

The Ministry

Dissatisfaction with the chapter on the ministry was prevalent at the Chicago Conferences. The reasons for dissatisfaction included a desire to represent more adequately the traditions of ministry from the Evangelical United Brethren Church and the Methodist Church, the impact of external studies of the ministry in the Consultation on Church Union and elsewhere, the first signs of restlessness about the status of deaconesses, and the fact that the Methodist General Conference of 1960 had appointed a commission to study the ministry and the Joint Commission on Union had engaged in a similar study. It was evident that the two commissions had come to conclusions which were dissimilar, if not contradictory. Consequently, the chapter "The Ministry" had to be rewritten.

The new study was conducted by a committee that combined the talents of the Methodist Commission on the Ministry appointed in 1960 and several Evangelical United Brethren leaders. Bishop James W. Henley and Bishop Paul W. Milhouse served as chairman and vice-chairman, respectively, and Dr. K. Morgan Edwards served as secretary. Under their gracious and skillful leadership, the commission had a vigorous and productive experience in the development of the new chapter. The commission included the following persons:

Methodists	Evangelical United Brethren
James W. Henley, Chairman	Paul W. Milhouse, Vice-Chairman
K. Morgan Edwards, Secretary	E. Craig Brandenburg
William F. Case	Paul H. Eller
Charles B. Copher	John Knecht
Graham S. Eubank	Q. C. Lansman
Earl H. Ferguson	Millard J. Miller
Edwin R. Garrison	Gene Sease
L. D. Havighurst	W. Maynard Sparks
Carl F. Lueg	Paul Washburn
Gerald O. McCulloh	
Bradshaw Mintner	
Harold T. Porter	
C. Jasper Smith	
Mack B. Stokes	
Jack M. Tuell	
John R. VanSickle	
D. Frederick Wertz	

The chapter on the ministry, as we shall see in the next chapter, like the chapter on the local church, held promise for the renewal of the church while preserving a definition of ministry that could be considered faithful to the traditions of the uniting churches. In legislative process the Uniting Conference would be required to wrestle with renewal.

The Program Council

Known in 1980 as the Council on Ministries and existing at four levels—the general, the jurisdictional, the Annual Conference, and the local church—this council has lived under the shadow of one major question. How much power shall it have? When discussing the power granted to the General Council on Ministries, the questions run in two directions. First, how much power should the General Council on Ministries have in relation to the General Council on Finance and Administration and the Council of Bishops? Second, how much power should the council have in relation to the General Program Boards of the church? This council holds great potential for the church once its areas of responsibility are clearly defined and in place among the power forces of the church. There is little hope of doing away with the struggle for power in the church, or any place else for that matter where humans are concerned; but there is hope of building checks and balances around powers and hope for the refinement of the covenants under which all persons and agencies can operate in relative peace.

Charles Parlin served as chairman and the Reverend Paul Church served as secretary of the committee of the Joint Commission, which tried to find the right structure and the proper arena for the operation of this agency.

The Board of Laity

Mr. Leonard Sorg, president of Evangelical United Brethren Men, served as chairman of the Committee on the Board of Laity and Mr. Lloyd M. Berthoff, former president of Illinois Wesleyan University, served as secretary. Twelve strong laymen were members of this committee as were seven strong clergymen. They planned a board to operate through two divisions: (1) a Division of Lay Life and Work and (2) a Division of Stewardship and Finance. A fallacy built into the consciousness of this board was its failure to envision women as part of the *laos*. Even their statement of objective was wider than their practice. It said:

The board believes the basic objective of the church is that **all** persons be aware of and grow in their understanding of God, especially of his redeeming love as revealed in Jesus Christ, and that they respond in faith and love—to the end that they may know who they are and what their human situation means, increasingly identify themselves as **sons** of God and members of the Christian community, live in the spirit of God in every relationship, fulfill their common discipleship in the world, and abide in Christian hope.[2]

As the Dallas Uniting Conference drew nearer, the commissioners grew ever more aware of the limitations of their plans. Criticisms from several sources helped to sharpen the areas of inadequacy and inspired plans for commissions to continue the development of the church beyond the Uniting Conference. Charles Parlin proposed to the Joint Commission the appointment of four much-needed commissions: (1) a Creedal Statement Commission, (2) a Social Principles Study Commission, (3) a Structure Study Commission, and (4) a Commission of Structure of Methodism Overseas. His proposals not only identified clearly what the commissions were to do, but they suggested plans for membership on them. His rationale was so realistic in terms of the Joint Commission's unfinished business that the proposals were readily adopted and referred to the Uniting Conference for implementation.

A report of 165 pages setting forth thirty-three revisions of Part IV and nine resolutions was published and delivered to all the delegates to the Uniting Conference by February 15, 1968. Delegates had ample opportunity to do their homework before coming to Dallas.

Interpretation of the Plan

A publication that aided the constituencies of the churches in their understanding of the Plan of Union was a pamphlet written by Bishop Lloyd C. Wicke of the Methodist Church and Bishop Reuben H. Mueller of the Evangelical United Brethren Church. This piece, published by the Women's Division of the Methodist Board of Missions, was entitled *One Spirit*. It declared, "The idea of union is based on the fundamental oneness of the body of Christ. Fractures in the body of Christ, among the members of the families of kindred spirits should not continue."

One Spirit was unique in that it dedicated its last page to questions women were asking:

Question: What are the provisions for the Women's Division?

Answer: The Women's Division shall include responsibilities formerly carried by the Woman's Society of Christian Service of The Methodist Church and the Women's Society of World Service of The Evangelical United Brethren Church. The scope of the Division in the Board of Missions shall be rooted in the concerns of the church in today's world, including special needs and interests of women. It shall foster spiritual growth and missionary outreach.

Question: How will it be organized?

Answer: The Women's Division shall be organized into three sections—namely, the Section of Program and Education for Christian Mission, the Section of Christian Social Relations, and the Section of Finance.

Question: How will the work of women be financed?

Answer: By annual voluntary pledges, special memberships, special offerings, bequests and annuities.

Question: What about the annual conference Women's Society of Christian Service?

Answer: In each annual conference there shall be organized a conference Women's Society of Christian Service, auxiliary to the jurisdiction Women's Society of Christian Service and to the General Board of Missions through the Women's Division. Its purpose will be to unite the women of the church in Christian fellowship to make Christ known throughout the world: to develop a personal responsibility for the whole task of the church, to plan and direct the work of the society within the conference.

Question: Will there be a Wesleyan Service Guild?

Answer: Yes.

Question: Will there be a local Women's Society of Christian Service?

Answer: Most definitely![3]

The Joint Commission published another pamphlet entitled *Helps for Voting on The Plan of Union to form The United Methodist Church* and a biweekly piece entitled *Light on the Way*. The first of these was widely distributed and answered important questions about the union. For instance, one question posed was: "What is the position of The United Methodist Church and racial integration?" The answer:

The Constitution, Division One, Article IV, defines The United Methodist Church as an inclusive church and provides that no conference or other organizational unit of the church shall be structured so as to exclude any member or any constituent body of the church because of race, color, national origin, or economic condition. It also specifically provides that there shall be no Jurisdictional or Central Conference based on any ground other than geographical and regional division; that definition of church membership must in every case be without reference to race or status; and that the General Conference has the authority to secure the rights and privileges of membership in all agencies, programs, and institutions in the church regardless of race or status. The Enabling Legislation records the intention that union shall in no way delay or impede, but rather facilitate, strengthen, encourage and hasten elimination of any racial structure of disctinction.[4]

Another question: "What should be the determing factor or factors in deciding how to vote in the annual conferences?" The answer:

The Plan of Union is not perfect. It does, however, represent years of patient effort by Joint Commissions duly appointed by their respective churches and a careful review and debate in the two General Conferences. It is safe to assume that every delegate would have made some changes if that delegate, alone, had had the sole right to do the drafting.

In voting, it must come to a question of relative importance. Each delegate must determine: Is it right that my church should move forward in a move toward Christian unity? If so, are the questioned points in the Plan so important that the Plan should be rejected?[5]

Light on the Way, slanted in favor of union, written almost entirely by Paul Washburn, began in its first issue with the theological foundations for Christian unity. One paragraph in that first issue set the tone for the publication:

Rudolph Schiele in addressing the Evangelical United Brethren General Conference about Methodist Evangelical United Brethren union negotiations in Germany said: "We have found our Lord between us." So it may be for us in America! If we try to put our own ways of believing and acting in the middle as requirement for the unity of Christ's people we will not receive unity. We will fall short of unity because our personal beliefs and experiences can not be normative for all. The One Christ, who is beyond, central and authoritative, is our unity.[6]

At the request of the Evangelical United Brethren Commission, Paul Washburn had visited every Annual Conference in that church in 1966. In 1967 he did it again, delivering an address entitled "Where Is the Promised Land?" The address spoke of values and disvalues attendant upon saying no to union and about the values and disvalues attendant upon saying yes to union. This address was delivered before the Annual Conferences voted on the union.

Voting in Annual Conferences

Amendments to Constitutional Law of the Evangelical United Brethren Church and to the Constitution of the Methodist Church required approval by General Conferences and second approval by Annual Conferences. These provisions in the Constitutions state, "Amendments to the Constitution shall be made upon a two-thirds majority vote of the General Conference present and voting, and a two-thirds affirmative vote of the aggregate number of members of the several Annual Conferences and Missionary Conferences present and voting."

Readers will recall that on November 11, 1966, the Evangelical United Brethren General Conference gained a 78.6 percent majority for union and that the Methodist General Conference gained a 94.9 percent majority for union. Both those desiring this union and those opposed to it watched and counted with interest the votes in Annual Conferences.

The vote in Methodist Annual Conferences showed that those conferences would vote the union early in the summer of 1967. Only nine conferences did not gain a two-thirds majority, and all of the nine were southern conferences. The final tally showed 30,781 votes in the affirmative and 4,197 votes in the negative, representing a vote of 88 percent in favor of union.

The vote in Evangelical United Brethren Conferences took a little longer. With thirty-two conferences voting, the union hung in the balances of indecision until the thirty-first conference voted—the Ohio Sandusky Conference. Twelve of the thirty-two conferences failed to gain a two-thirds majority. The final tally showed 3,740 votes for union and 1,606 against union, or an aggregate majority in the affirmative of 69.9 percent.

Agreements had been made between the two commissions that, in the event union was approved, the presiding bishops from the two churches would have the privilege of announcing the good news. Late in the afternoon of June 26, 1967, when union was assured, Bishop Donald H. Tippett was somewhere in North Carolina and could not be found, and Bishop Reuben

H. Mueller was in Europe and could not be reached. So the announcement was made in another way. Mr. Tom Moore, a member of the Ohio Sandusky Conference, owned and operated a radio station in Bucyrus, Ohio. When the results of the voting were announced by Bishop Paul M. Herrick, Mr. Moore knew that union was assured and used the facilities at his command to make the announcement of the union.

Methodist Information carried the glad line on June 27, 1967, "Union of The Methodist Church and The Evangelical United Brethren Church is now a statistical certainty."

An Episcopal Declaration by the Board of the Evangelical United Brethren Church closed with the following paragraph:

For this achievement under God, we express our thanks to Him, invoking at the same time the guidance of the Holy Spirit as we, together with The Methodist Church, prepare for this union, to the glory of Jesus Christ our Lord and the strengthening of His Church. Basic throughout these union negotiations has been a united yearning for spiritual renewal so that the Church may be baptized afresh with divine fires and endued with the necessary spiritual vision and resources in Christ to meet the challenges and needs of the times in which we live and of the world of which we are a part. We earnestly urge men and women everywhere to lift up dedicated hand and hearts in prayer and service to the end that The United Methodist Church will truly be Christ's Church.

At a subsequent meeting of the Joint Commission, Dr. Norman Trott prayed, "We have come a long way together and Thou hast been with us. We look with joy to the future where in one united fellowship we will seek to perfect the church Thou hast given. Amen."

An Attempt at Reconciliation

Persons who were opposed to the union were numerous in four Annual Conferences of the Evangelical United Brethren Church: the Erie Conference, the Montana Conference, the Northwest Canada Conference, and the Pacific Northwest Conference (which included Oregon and Washington). Arguments supporting their opposition were basically theological in nature. As early as the Grand Rapids General Conference in 1962, the Montana and Pacific Northwest Conferences presented resolutions that, if adopted, would have allowed those conferences to secede from the church in the event of union. Sensing the estrangement that was growing between these opponents of the union and the rest of the church, the General Conference of 1966 appointed a Commission on Unity and charged it to seek reconciliation with these opponents of union. Failing to gain reconciliation, the commission was charged to arrange financial settlements with the Montana and Pacific Northwest Conferences.

The Reverend Warren Mentzer was chairman of the commission, and Paul

Washburn was secretary. Two laymen, Elmer Funkhouser and Rolland Osborne, and two other clergypersons, Marvin Leist and Bishop W. Maynard Sparks, were the other members of the commission. These men went directly into the geographical locations of the opposition on two occasions. Meetings were cordial and well ordered emotionally, but there was to be no relenting on the part of the opposition. The commission informed the dissidents that individual ministers could withdraw from the denomination and that individual members could do likewise but that congregations could not withdraw from the connection nor could an entire conference withdraw.

In both Montana and the Pacific Northwest, significant minorities were for the union and wanted to become part of The United Methodist Church; thus, they had a right to the properties.

Bishop W. Maynard Sparks, who was the presiding bishop over both of these conferences, stood tall in his ministrations to them. At the height of the conflict he said to these conferences:

I am glad to be a part of the Commission on Union. Like many of you it was a distinct privilege to participate actively in the church union efforts of the forties. In intercessions, in commission and committee work, in writing and speaking, and in voluminous amounts of correspondence I have tried to give myself to the calls that have come to me. If the decision makers of The Methodist and The Evangelical United Brethren General Conferences of 1966 vote favorably to what is presented and those of 1967 add their undergirding I shall give myself in all that I can do to make effective such a union in the few years of active service that may remain. If the decision makers are not led to favor such a union at this time I shall do all in my power wheresoever my station in life may be to make strong the witness to advance for our Lord through the denominational pattern of which we are a part.

There is a Person—a most important Person—who must never be by-passed by any of us. He is the Lord of the Church. Long before any of us came on the scene He was at work. In strange and varied ways He is quite busy today in the hearts of men and movements and long after we pass from the scene of mortal action He will be here. I have full confidence in Him. I have confidence in His children both in the Methodist and Evangelical United Brethren families. Though there are many cross currents in our thinking—and who is free from such—and though confusion rises in high tide on more than one occasion (and this is not at all bad by any means) I believe the faithful will hear God's voice and heed it. What more dare I ask? What more can I ask? Lord hear our prayers today. Thy will be done.[7]

Through the efforts of the Commission on Unity, in both Montana and the Pacific Northwest those ministers and church members who desired them were granted transfers of memberships to the Evangelical Church of North America. For about $700,000 in the Pacific Northwest and for about $70,000 in Montana, those members who transferred to the new denomination were permitted to buy the church buildings and parsonages they were occupying. It was a sad experience to sit one day in a Portland,

Oregon, church and witness seventy-three ministers come forth to request transfer of their credentials to the Evangelical Church of North America.

In the *Handbook of Denominations in The United States,* the Evangelical Church of North America reports 11,909 members in 137 congregations. Our venture in unity is not complete.

A few congregations around Erie, Pennsylvania, joined the Evangelical Church of North America and the Northwest Canada Conference became an Affiliated Autonomous Church and joined the Evangelical Church of North America in 1982.

Making Ready

Numerous tasks had to be performed in preparation for The United Methodist Church. Committees were appointed to develop Guidelines for Integration of Board and Agency Personnel, Guidelines for Housing of Agencies, Guidelines for Unification of Boards and Agencies, Guidelines for Unification of Annual Conferences, Guidelines for Unification of Local Churches, Budget for the new quadrennium, and a Committee on Quadrennial Emphasis. Never was there more elaborate preparation for the coming together of two churches.

10

The Dallas Uniting Conference—1968

Two Last Days

April 22, 1968, was the last day of the Evangelical United Brethren Church and the last day of the Methodist Church, for from April 23, 1968, onward these two churches, without forgetting the timbers of heritage from which they were hewn, would continue their existence as The United Methodist Church. On that last day the uniting churches held separate and final sessions of their General Conferences to put closure on their separate existences and to prepare themselves for taking a new pilgrimage together.

Last Day for the Methodists

The General Conference of the Methodist Church met in the Crystal Ballroom of the Baker Hotel in Dallas, Texas. Bishop Donald H. Tippett of the San Francisco Area presided.

Bishop R. Marvin Stuart led in the devotional period. He invited retired Bishop Arthur Moore to pray. The concluding paragraph of Bishop Moore's prayer was memorable:

We thank thee, God, for our approaching fellowship with our comrades of the Evangelical United Brethren Church. Grant to us in our approaching, Heavenly Father, a more intimate fellowship with our Lord. Never allow us to despair of the world's redemption or to run away from the problems of the earth. Give us a more tenacious hold upon the everlasting certainties of our faith and help us, with those certainties, to initiate a great spiritual offensive. Save us from fear, from futility and from despair. Deliver us from temporizing and shallow makeshift. Sustain us with an eager expectancy of the soul. Let our hearts glow this day and in all the coming days with a faith in the ultimate triumph of our Blessed Lord. Never allow us to mistake the clatter of the ecclesiastical machinery for the winds of heaven. Help us to march to our task as a world church not with crutch and bandage but with the sound of trumpets and marching feet. Send us before long another great spiritual awakening of quickening power and let it begin with us for Christ's sake. Amen.[1]

Bishop Stuart said during his sermon:

115

Certainly we want the tone of this especially important General Conference, with an historic union about to be consummated, to be one of affirmation and hope, I should like not to spend our entire time together in criticism and dissent. Yet, unless we grapple with the issues at the heart, not only of our life as a church, but our life together as a total society and as the family of man, we might as well close up our attache cases and go home right now. A nation engaged in a bloody and costly war in Asia, in rioting and assassination in its streets at home, and with a growth of doubt and despair spreading like disease throughout its entire social fabric, requires a church that is alive.[2]

The agenda for the day included: a report from the Council of Bishops on the vote on union by Bishop Short; a report from Bishop Raines and Dr. Merrill Powers on the Quadrennial Emphasis; a report on the Advance from Bishop Werner; a report from the Commission on Promotion and Cultivation by Dr. Howard Greenwalt; a report from the Judicial Council by its president, Mr. Paul R. Ervin; a report from the Coordinating Council by Bishop Mathews; a report of the World Family Life Movement by Bishop Werner; and a report from the Ad Hoc Committee on Union by Dr. Charles Parlin.

The conference adjourned to assemble again in the evening to hear the Episcopal Address delivered by Bishop Lloyd C. Wicke.

Last Day for the Evangelical United Brethren

The Adjourned Session of the 1966 General Conference of the Evangelical United Brethren Church met in the Little Theater of the Memorial Auditorium in Dallas, Texas. Bishop Harold R. Heininger presided. In his Episcopal Message, Bishop Reuben H. Mueller said:

One of the most important actions we will need to take is to consider the request for retirement from active service by our colleague, Bishop H. R. Heininger, and to elect a new bishop to succeed him.[3]
This entire enterprise in union has been a venture of daring faith in discovering and obeying God's will for our churches, from its very inception ten years ago. Every step has been taken according to the provisions of the *Disciplines* of our two denominations, which specify ways whereby the majority will of our connectional denominations come to mature expression. At the same time, minority positions were permitted free expression, according to the same constitutional provisions. There has been some questioning, some opposition, some wavering in loyalty to the denomination, but in spite of these the cause of church union advanced steadily, step-by-step, in a spirit of questing for better ways of Christian discipleship and witnessing in the world-wide Christian fellowship.[4]

Dr. Warren Mentzer reported for the Commission on Unity that had been raised to seek reconciliation with the Montana, Northwest Canada, and Pacific Northwest Conferences where majorities of the members opposed union. Dr. Mentzer said in part:

We visited these conferences upon two occasions, we are heartened by the fact that there are those who still remain loyal to the church. These persons have been going through much difficulty and many troubles of order. We are heartbroken by what we have found and experienced. I trust God that even in this moment, when we still have no report of any mass withdrawals of members from any of the churches, that the minds and hearts of the peoples of the Pacific Northwest and Montana Conferences might be changed and that we might experience the unity which as a commission we sought to represent and express as representatives of this General Conference.[5]

In commending the Commission on Unity for its work, Bishop Heininger said: "You have interpreted on behalf of the entire church the desire for reconciliation, you have been mediating the love of Christ and when in a moment we approve your report we want to say thank you for the hours of prayer, listening and interpretation which you have contributed creatively to the on-going life of the church."[6] I have reported in chapter 9 the outcome of this venture in reconciliation.

The Enabling Legislation for the Union provided that the Evangelical United Brethren Church was to provide seven bishops for The United Methodist Church. After Bishop Heininger's request for retirement was granted, the conference cast a ballot for a bishop to be the seventh bishop from the Evangelical United Brethren Church, and the writer of this history was elected.

Evangelical United Brethren installed bishops. They did not consecrate them. In presiding over my installation, Bishop Mueller noted the importance of the moment, saying:

At the time when Mr. Francis Asbury, and I say Mr. Asbury because he was a layman when they started, was chosen to be one of the first bishops of The Methodist Episcopal Church and by a rapid process of ordination moved from deacon to elder to bishop in three days . . . when it came time for Asbury to be consecrated as bishop he insisted that Philip William Otterbein should be one of those who would be present for that consecration and would join in the laying on of hands. Now this ceremony of laying on of hands we do not have in our installation service, but I would like to at least repeat the compliment and even the story, and so I have invited the secretary of the Council of Bishops of The Methodist Church, Bishop Roy H. Short of Louisville, Kentucky, to come and share in this installation service. That ought to make both Asbury and Otterbein glad this afternoon as they are looking over the battlements and ramparts of heaven at what is going on in Dallas, Texas, during these days.[7]

I appreciated several gracious acts performed in behalf of my episcopacy on that April afternoon: the fact that Mrs. Washburn, our two daughters, one of our sons-in-law, and two of our grandsons were invited to sit close by during the service; the fact that Bishop Heininger who had been my professor of theology at Evangelical Theological Seminary, my parishioner for a time in Naperville, and my bishop for fourteen years read the charge; the fact that Bishop Roy H. Short came to read the lessons; the fact that Bishop Mueller examined me that day; and the fact that Bishop George Edward Epp, who had been my bishop from 1934 to 1950 and had ordained me both deacon and elder, offered the consecratory prayer. I have read and reread the pages describing the event in the *Daily Christian Advocate* to remind myself of what I promised to be and do.

All of the boards and agencies of the church reported that day through their chief executive officers. In a way there was sadness in the air as we thought of the ending of our small and intimate fellowship; but the sadness was interlaced with joy as we thought of the new relationships and responsibilities which lay before us in The United Methodist Church.

The Episcopal Message

On the eve of the celebration of union, which is described in the first chapter of this book, the Episcopal Address was delivered in behalf of the Council of Bishops by Bishop Lloyd C. Wicke. The opening greeting of that address set the mood, not only for the evening, but for the entire conference:

To the members of this Conference which shall unite The Evangelical United Brethren Church and The Methodist Church bringing into being The United Methodist Church; to laymen, to ministers, to friends, to casual observers, grace and peace from God our Father.

> Now thank we all our god
> With heart and hand and voices,
> Who wondrous things hath done,
> In whom his world rejoices;
> Who, from our mothers' arms,
> Hath blessed us on our way
> With countless gifts of love,
> And still is ours today.

Commenting early in the address on the union, Bishop Wicke moved quickly to rivet the attention of the gathered throng upon the work that lay ahead. He said:

This is the second occasion in Methodist history when the church gathered as a Uniting Conference. It marks the third such event in the life of the predecessor members of The Evangelical United Brethren Church.

In 1939 the Methodist bishops note that this "uniting conference . . . has no distinct precedent, and will have no distinct successor." Consequently the Episcopal Address was "framed with the dominant purpose of exalting the mission of a conference unique in Methodism.

The re-uniting of the strands of the former Evangelical Association in 1922 was marked by a sense of fraternal joy that a new way had been found to re-unite old friends. The union of The United Brethren in Christ and The Evangelical Church in

1946 provided a mountain-top experience when "the sun shown more brightly and the balmy atmosphere of Christian fellowship was never warmer."

Today's event should provide an opportunity to examine the work in past years, its present state, and what may be expected in the future.[8]

During this conference we must continually remind ourselves that yesterday's unfinished business becomes the clamouring first item on today's agenda. The penalty assessed against those who ignore these items is the visiting upon their children's children of those grievances intensified. Remembrance is the secret of redemption. More than remembrance is required, that "more" will challenge us over these days.[9]

The remainder of the address was a clarion call to The United Methodist Church to understand itself, to claim its vocation, to behold the city, to use the Bible, to claim its place in the wider Christian fellowship, to be responsible partners in the world parish, to witness in a Christian way through out institutions of higher learning, and to heed the cry of war. In conclusion, the message said:

In these hours we stand at a boundary. We are about to cross over a new land. We have spied it out and found it good. We bring possessions in abundance. Union having been achieved must now be husbanded in sincerity with grace.

As we cross the frontier many will carry a full measure of evangelistic inheritance. Apart from our continuing zeal which unceasingly seeks self-commitment to our Lord as the altar from which every heart should depart into the world, The United Methodist Church will become an impotent institution living on uneasily and uselessly, Christ's mission considered. Empowered by our commitment to Him that mission will not fail because He has never failed us.

In crossing the boundary others will not permit us to forget the full burden of our social responsibilities. The United Methodist Church will continue to pray, "O Lord, grant us a clear vision to perceive those things which in our social order are amiss, giving us true judgment, courage and perseverance to help right the injustices of our time, enduing each of us with wisdom and strength to minister to the poor, the suffering and the friendless, being Christ's friend to each of these." In part, our willed deed should become the answer to our prayer as through his grace working in us the lame will walk, the blind will see, the lonely will find a friend, and the sinner will find grace.[10]

To the Work

A Committee on Entertainment and Program can arrange the immediate circumstances of a General Conference and choose persons to serve as liturgists and preachers, the Council of Bishops can form an Episcopal Message and designate one of their number to write and deliver it, but the hard work of a General Conference is done in its legislative sections and plenary sessions. One editor observed that he expected the Dallas Uniting Conference to be a cautious, conservative, hold-the-line conference but found that the deliberations and actions of the conference ran quite counter to his expectation.

Part IV—Organization and Administration of the Plan of Union, which had been approved in principle at the Chicago Conferences of 1966, plus thirty-three revisions and nine resolutions recommended by the Joint Commission on Union, plus three thousand petitions, all destined to be considered as possible amendments to the plan, comprised the material to be worked through the legislative process. When that process was ended, the results became Part IV—Organization and Administration of *The Book of Discipline* and the body of covenants to guide the members, the congregations, the conferences, the boards and agencies, and the ministers and bishops of The United Methodist Church until further amended.

General Officers

One difficult but essential task was the determination of which executive posts would be held by former Evangelical United Brethren and which ones by former Methodists. A very small committee undertook the task of consultation with all of the persons involved and finally arrived at the following conclusion:

Board of Church and Society
General Secretary	A. Dudley Ward	(M)
Associate General Secretary	Grover Bagby	(M)
Associate General Secretary	C. Dale White	(M)
Associate General Secretary	Herman Wills	(M)

Board of Education
General Secretary, Editorial	Henry Bullock	(M)
Associate General Secretary	Harold Hazenfield	(E)
General Secretary, Higher Education	Myron Wicke	(M)
Associate General Secretary	E. Craig Brandenburg	(E)
General Secretary, Local Church	Howard Ham	(M)

Board of Evangelism
General Secretary	Joseph Yeakel	(E)

Board of Health and Welfare Ministries
General Secretary	Roger Burgess	(M)

Board of Laity
General Secretary	Vacancy	(M)

Board of Missions
General Secretary	Tracey Jones, Jr.	(M)
Associate General Secretary—World	John F. Schaefer	(E)

Associate General Secretary—National	Edward Carothers	(M)
Associate General Secretary—Women	Theressa Hoover	(M)
Associate General Secretary— Education and Cultivation	Lois Miller	(E)
Associate General Secretary—UMCOR	Harry Haines	(M)

Board of Pensions

| General Secretary | C. Claire Hoyt | (M) |
| Associate General Secretary | Harley Hiller | (E) |

Board of Publication

Publisher and President	Lovick Pierce	(M)
Vice President	Donald A. Theuer	(E)
Vice President	J. Otis Young	(M)
Vice President	Ewing Wayland	(M)
Editorial Director	Curtis Chambers	(E)

Program Council

General Secretary	Paul V. Church	(E)
Associate General Secretary	Gerald Clapsaddle	(M)
Associate General Secretary	Howard Greenwalt	(M)
Associate General Secretary	Harry Spencer	(M)

Commission on Archives and History

| General Secretary | T. Otto Nall | (M) |
| Associate General Secretary | John Ness | (E) |

Commission on Chaplains

| General Secretary | John McLaughlin | (M) |

Commission on Ecumenical Affairs

| General Secretary | Robert Huston | (M) |

Commission on United Methodist Information

| General Secretary | Arthur West | (M) |

Council on World Service and Finance

| General Secretary | R. Bryan Brawner | (M) |

Only one of the above executives declined to serve in the office for which he had been selected. All other personnel of the boards and agencies of both churches were given positions in the united church excepting only those who declined to serve in the posts offered. It is interesting to note that in 1984—sixteen years after union—only three of the thirty-five persons listed above still occupied the same office and only six of them have not retired. The completion of this task took a large amount of pressure off the Dallas Conference.

Headquarters for Agencies

In order to coordinate personnel and ministries with counterpart personnel and ministries of The Methodist Church, all but one of the Evangelical United Brethren boards and agencies were required to leave Dayton, Ohio, the one center of the Evangelical United Brethren Church, and to move either to Evanston, Illinois, to Lake Junaluska, North Carolina; to Nashville, Tennessee, to New York City, or to Washington, D. C. Only the General Program Council (now the General Council of Ministries) and the General Commission on Public Relations and Information (now the General Commission on Communications) were headquartered in the General Offices Building of the Evangelical United Brethren Church in Dayton.

Only a modicum of imagination is required in order to understand the trauma experienced by the Evangelical United Brethren constituency in the Dayton area, which had become accustomed to thinking of itself as central, and by the general officers who had to leave their homes, churches, and civic responsibilities in order to continue their ministries. It was trauma somewhat like the trauma that would attend any attempt to scatter Mecca to the four winds. If one listens carefully today, one can still hear the sounds of nostalgia in the words and voices of the old-timers of the Evangelical United Brethren Church. The coordination of headquarters of boards and agencies, however, was of the essence of union.

Actions of the Uniting Conference

Delegates to the Uniting Conference seemed to have heard a call to action in Dr. Outler's sermon, "The Unfinished Business of an Unfinished Church." Instead of hearing that sermon as a realistic definition of any church this side of the eschaton, the delegates in legislative and plenary sessions worked diligently to finish the unfinished business or to present to the world a less unfinished church. Now, sixteen years after union, it does appear that the actions addressing the unfinished business of the church were more productive of revitalization of the church than were the actions seeking to finish an unfinished church. Perhaps the delegates to that conference should have been reminded of Emil Brunner's comment, "The Church exists by mission as a fire exists by burning."

Some actions of the Uniting Conference took effect immediately while others were to impact the church only after special commissions had done extensive research and reported findings to subsequent General Conferences. It is, at least, presumptuous to describe the most significant actions of that Uniting Conference. Whether or not the actions described in the following pages were the most significant, and whether or not the actions addressed the unfinished business or the unfinished church, must be left for the readers to decide.

Action on the Local Church

Vigorous sentences in *The Book of Discipline—1968* speak of the theological importance of the local church: "A local church is a community of true believers under the Lordship of Christ. The Church of Jesus Christ exists in and for the world. The local church is a connectional society of persons who have professed their faith in Jesus Christ. A member of any local United Methodist Church is a member of the total United Methodist connection. The United Methodist Church, a fellowship of believers, is a part of the Church Universal. Therefore, all persons, without regard to race, color, national origin, or economic condition, shall be eligible to attend its worship services, to participate in its program, and, when they take the appropriate vows, to be admitted into membership in any local church in the connection. A member of The United Methodist Church is to be a servant on mission in the local and worldwide community. This servanthood is performed in family life, daily work, recreation and social activities, responsible citizenship, the issues of corporate life, and in all attitudes toward persons."[11]

The internalization of these ideals by members and congregations of The United Methodist Church is a never-ending process that revitalizes the church.

Certain minimal ecclesiastical requirements are required of every local church. It shall hold a Charge Conference annually at the call of the District Superintendent which conference relates the local church to the total connection of The United Methodist Church. It shall have an Administrative Board that sets goals, initiates plans, authorizes actions, determines policy, receives reports, and reviews the state of the church. It shall have a Council on Ministries that initiates, develops, and coordinates the church's strategy for mission. It shall have a Nominating Committee that nominates persons for election to office in the local church. It shall have a Pastor-Parish Relations Committee to facilitate good relationships between pastor and parish through consultation and support. Probably, in these times of highly developed organizations in the secular sphere, these ecclesiastical requirements are better understood and therefore more effective than are the theological statements delineated above.

Recognizing that The United Methodist Church would embrace about 39,000 congregations of which approximately 27,000 would have less than 150 members, the Special Study Committee of the Methodist Interboard Commission on the Local Church and the Joint Committee on the Local Church of the Joint Commission of Church Union worked to define meanings and methods for the local church that would be applicable to congregations of all sizes. In adopting the chapter, "The Local Church," for inclusion in *The Book of Discipline,* the Uniting Conference provided definitions to enhance the theological meanings and the institutional methods of local churches. Ultimately, the meaning and the methods must be wedded in local churches desiring to be the church alive.

Action on the Ministry

Just as meanings and methods prescribed for the identification and functions of local churches hold promise of renewal, the definitions and orders for ministry promise renewal. Massive revisions of ways both laity and clergy thought, and still think, about ministry were, and are, required of those who accept the definitions and orders set forth in *The Book of Discipline—1968.* The revisions are called for in two paragraphs of the chapter, "The Ministry." These paragraphs have remained unchanged for four quadrennia, but it will take much longer to gain their acceptance by all the ministers of the church.

One paragraph indicated states:

Ministry in the Christian church is derived from the ministry of Christ, the ministry of the Father through the Incarnate Son by the Holy Spirit. It is a ministry bestowed upon and required of the entire church. All Christians are called to ministry, and theirs is a ministry of the people of God within the community of faith and in the world. Members of The United Methodist Church receive this gift of ministry in company with all Christians and sincerely hope to continue and extend it in the world for which Christ lived, died and lives again. The United Methodist Church believes that baptism, confirmation and responsible membership in the Church are visible signs of acceptance of this ministry.[12]

So, the ministry of Christ is bestowed upon the *laos,* the whole people of God. Individual Christians may receive the gift of Christ's ministry and may say, "I am a minister." Groups of Christians may receive the gift of Christ's ministry and may say, "We are ministers." But claiming to be ministers is not the same as being ministers. Ministry permeates ministers, their personalities, their vocations, their avocations, their citizenship, and their relationships in families, in communities, and in churches. At base, ministry is the gift of Christ and is intended to imbue, to infiltrate, to impregnate, to permeate, and to pervade individuals and groups who receive the gift. What would have happened if the 11 million United Methodists who claimed membership in The United Methodist Church in 1968 had been pervaded with Christ's ministry?

The second definitive paragraph provides for ordained ministers. It states: "There are persons within the ministry of the baptized who are called of God and set apart by the Church for the specialized ministry of Word, Sacrament, and Order."[13]

Ordained ministers, who come most readily to mind when ministers are mentioned, "are persons within the ministry of the baptized." They are ministers in part because all Christians are ministers. They share the ministry of the *laos*. Bishop George Edward Epp told of a clergyman in Pennsylvania who tried to explain his failure in the ordained ministry by saying, "I could enjoy ministry if it were not for the people." The reality of ordained ministry is that it is ministry shared with other Christians. There is, perhaps, a difference of intensity but not in kind.

Ordained ministers "are called of God . . . for the specialized ministry of Word, Sacrament, and Order." United Methodists desire to test persons to ascertain if they are truly called of God to specialized ministries. The test questions, still used by the church, are questions used by John Wesley in 1746 to test Methodist preachers:

> 1. Do they know God as a pardoning God? Have they the love of God abiding in them? Do they desire nothing but God? Are they holy in all manner of conversation?
> 2. Have they gifts, as well as grace, for the work? Have they a clear, sound understanding; a right judgment in the things of God; a just conception of salvation by faith? Do they speak justly, readily, clearly?
> 3. Have they fruit? Have any been truly convinced of sin and converted to God, and are believers edified by their preaching?

As long as these marks concur in anyone, we believe he is called of God to preach. These we receive as sufficient proof that he is moved by the Holy Spirit.

Ordained ministers are "set apart (set into) by the Church for the specialized ministry of Word, Sacrament, and Order." Planting the seed of the living Word in fields of congregation and world is one of the specialized tasks of ordained ministers, but the seed of the living Word is available for all other Christians to plant also. Presiding at celebrations of the sacraments is another specialized task of ordained ministers, but sacraments are meaningless without the participation of other Christians. Fostering order in the church is the other specialized task of ordained ministers, but that order comes voluntarily. It cannot be coerced. Even the specialized tasks of ordained ministers are dependent upon the cooperation of congregations.

Two orders of clergy are provided: deacons and elders. All deacons and elders are required, for the sake of accountability, to hold membership in an Annual Conference. There are three classifications of members: probationary, associate, and full.

By adopting these definitions and orders of ministry, the Uniting Conference opened the possibility of revitalization of the church. That conference pointed the way for the church to exist by functioning ministry as fire exists by burning.

Movements, some of them of long-standing and some of them of more recent origin, kept, and still keep, pressure on the church's thoughts about ministry. One long-term pressure rises out of the attempt of laymen and laywomen to wrest from the clergy the right to speak, to vote, and to share in the serving offices in the councils of the church. A second pressure comes from the desire of women for equal access with men to every role and office in the church. This pressure was exerted at the time of union by requests from deaconesses for certain rights in the church. A third pressure came from the ecumenical movement, especially the Consultation on Church Union, where some voices were clamoring, with futility, for the elimination of the practice of ordination. These movements were present and exerted pressure on the thoughts of those who wrote the sentences from *The Book of Discipline* lifted above—sentences carrying more promise for the revitalization of the church's ministry than has yet been realized.

Action on the Inclusive Church

Article IV in Division One of the Constitution, adopted by the General Conferences in Chicago on November 11, 1966, and by Annual Conferences throughout the uniting churches in their sessions of 1967, declared The United Methodist Church to be an inclusive church and made it unconstitutional for any conference or other organizational unit of the church to be structured so as to exclude any member of any constituent body because of race, color, national origin, or economic condition. The adoption of this amendment eliminated the Central Jurisdiction and put pressure on all segregated Annual Conferences to unite but, alas, the amendment did not eliminate racism in The United Methodist Church.

The elimination of the Central Jurisdiction and the assignment of all Central Jurisdiction bishops to integrated episcopal areas in the geographical jurisdictions were accomplished at the Uniting Conference. The provision for the action in the Enabling Legislation states, "The bishops originally elected by the Central Jurisdiction of The Methodist Church and not already assigned shall be assigned so that there shall be (from the Central Jurisdiction) one bishop in the Southeastern Jurisdiction and one bishop in the South Central Jurisdiction and one bishop in the Western Jurisdiction." In these two actions, The United Methodist Church acted like an inclusive church, but not even these actions eliminated racism in The United Methodist Church.

Realizing that racism was a demonic force in the church that could be exorcised only with the passage of time and with diligent effort by a responsible church and the grace of God, the Uniting Conference created a Commission on Religion and Race. Responsibilities were assigned to this new commission:

1. Supervision and administration of a general fund set up to assist mergers of predominantly white and black annual conferences;
2. Facilitate the merging of such conferences;
3. Counsel and encourage local churches which are seeking to become truly inclusive fellowships;
4. Cooperate with other black denominations;

5. Coordinate denominational support and cooperation with various prophetic movements for racial and social justice;

6. Help to assure participation by blacks and other minority group members on every level of the church's life and ministry;

7. Help to set up convocations of religion and race at all levels of the church.

8. Assist in the total program of The United Methodist Church designed to develop a racially inclusive church, including interracial pastors schools and the opening of all churches for worship to all without regard to race or ethnic background.

The creation of the Commission on Religion and Race proved to be a faithful act and a prophetic act by the Uniting Conference. It was a faithful act because it addressed one of the most grievous sins in the fabric of the church's life. It was a prophetic act because its formation provided precedent for the formation of another commission designed to address another grievous sin in the church's life. That other agency is the Commission on the Status and Role of Women.

Action Granting Autonomy to Twenty-seven Overseas Churches

The Commission on the Structure of Methodism Overseas reported to the Uniting Conference requests from twenty-seven overseas Annual Conferences for structural independence from the new denomination. The granting of these requests would diminish the membership of the church by more than a half million members. Bishop Richard C. Raines, president of the commission, said: "All the requests are either to permit overseas churches to form regional autonomous Methodist churches or to enter united churches." He added: "All the conferences have expressed a desire to continue to be related to The United Methodist Church in the United States through an affiliated autonomous status and to receive mission funds and personnel through the Board of Missions."

Requests to enter unions bent upon forming national churches came from conferences in Belgium, Hong Kong, India, Pakistan, and Sierra Leone. Requests to become autonomous Methodist churches came from Argentina, Bolivia, Chile, Costa Rica, Malaysia-Singapore, Panama, Peru, and Uruguay. Only the conferences in India did not carry out their original intentions, but in 1981 those conferences formed the Methodist Church of India and became an autonomous church affiliated with The United Methodist Church.

By granting the requests of these churches in fourteen countries, The United Methodist Church voted to become much less a world church. Basic reasons given for changing relationships with The United Methodist Church included the following: the desire for self-determination in the life and work of overseas churches, the desire to be missionary-sending churches as well as missionary-receiving churches, the appeal of a more ecumenical approach to the church's life through the formation of national churches, the rising tide of nationalism in many of the countries where these churches lived and worked, the conviction that the World Methodist Council provides an adequate vehicle for cooperation in mission for churches of the Wesleyan persuasion, and the conviction, held by a few persons, that the time had come for The United Methodist Church to declare its autonomy and become a national church.

Those who were opposed to granting the requests for autonomy argued that in times of rising tides of nationalism a world church is even more essential, that granting autonomy might mean the abandonment of those churches to whom it was granted, and that it would be possible for The United Methodist Church to become a partner in mission with churches that had been mission outposts without granting them autonomy.

The problem was, and is, very complex. At the close of World War II, Dr. Paul S. Mayer, an Evangelical Church missionary to Japan, was the first missionary to return to Japan. His return was facilitated because he belonged to a world church. Bishop Friedrich Wunderlich believed that he was able to function as the bishop in both East and West Germany because he had the support of a world church. In a wider sense, perhaps The United Methodist Church needs to see its relationships to all other churches not as a sovereign world body but as a servant body in league with all other servants of the world's people.

The church in Sierra Leone was among those churches requesting autonomy in 1968. Their request was granted. In less than a decade, messages began to come from that church requesting structural relationship with The United Methodist Church. Early in 1981 the affiliated autonomous church of Sierra Leone, at its Annual Conference session and at its General Conference session, approved the following resolutions:

1. That the conference accepts and approves the Constitution, Articles of Faith, the Discipline and Polity of The United Methodist Church.
2. Declare the Constitution of the Church of Sierra Leone null and void for the purpose of ecclesiastical union and relationship with The United Methodist Church.
3. That these decisions shall become effective only when The West Africa Central Conference is organized and constituted with two annual conferences, the Sierra Leone Annual Conference and the Liberia Annual Conference, and with Bishops T. S. Bangura and Arthur F. Kulah as its bishops, assigned to the Sierra Leone Area and the Liberia Area, respectively.

Bishop Ole Borgen, who had represented The United Methodist Church during the formation of the West Africa Central Conference, said in his report to the bishops of the church, "The Council of Bishops welcomes this addition to The United Methodist Church and rejoices in the strengthening of its witness in Africa and around the world."

While The United Methodist Church may be somewhat less a world church because autonomy was granted to twenty-eight Annual Conferences in fourteen countries at the Uniting Conference, the new church rejoiced in the independence of those conferences and welcomed the opportunity to become a partner in mission with them. Now, more than a decade later, The United Methodist Church along with the autonomous churches receives missionaries and sends missionaries. Thus, a more complete perception of the gospel becomes possible as that gospel, filtered through other cultures, is both spoken and heard by the partners in mission. Actually, a meshwork of good news begins to surround the globe, and even the proudest among us may hear a more complete gospel than we have heard before.

Decision to Study Structure

The Joint Commission on Union, as it approached the Uniting Conference, knew of clamoring in the church for more drastic revision of the structure of the church's boards and agencies than the Joint Commission and its subcommittee had been able to achieve. Three major achievements were, nevertheless, in place. The commission had been able to arrange for the correlation of the ministries of parallel agencies of the uniting churches, to arrange for the merging of parallel agencies in common headquarters, and to arrange for executive leadership of the agencies. Thus, the connectional ministries of the church continued uninterrupted under competent leadership. These were essential achievements.

Arguments for more drastic restructuring of the church included the following: the agency structure needs to be more flexible; the agencies need to be more relevant with a capacity to respond more promptly to calls for ministry; the agencies need to be more responsive to Annual Conferences and local churches; responsibilities for ministries and the resources required for the performance of those ministries need to be more equally divided among the agencies; there are still too many interboard councils challenging the concept and function of the Program Council; and the Program Council needs further development.

The Uniting Conference recognized the cogency of these and other arguments and voted to appoint a Structure Study Commission, saying:

1. There shall be a Structure Study Commission appointed with authorization to study thoroughly the board and agency structure of The United Methodist Church and to bring to the General Conference its recommendation for structuring of the boards and agencies of the church.
2. The Study Commission is authorized, in its discretion, to hold hearings in

various places in an effort to ascertain the needs of the local churches and how the witness and mission of the local church may become more relevant and effective.
3. The Study Commission is directed to work in consultation with the Council of Secretaries and the responsible officers of the various boards and agencies.

The Commission on Structure, composed of twenty-two persons, elected the Reverend Dow Kirkpatrick of Evanston, Illinois, as its chairperson and the Reverend Joel McDavid of Mobile, Alabama, as its secretary. The Reverend Paul McCleary was seconded by the Board of Missions to serve the commission as executive secretary.

Decision to Study Creedal Statements

One of the foremost arguments against the Plan of Union advanced by persons who were either against the union or wanted to postpone it contended that the union was not theologically based. Some opponents argued that a new creedal statement should have been worked out. Professors of theology and pastors from both chuches spearheaded this argument and far outnumbered laypersons who exhibited this concern.

Not only in the final attempt at union, which began in earnest in 1956, but in all previous attempts at union, leaders of the movements, often including outstanding theologians, agreed that there were no creedal impediments to union. In a paper presented to the Joint Commission of Union in 1958, Bishop Harold R. Heininger, who had been professor of systematic theology at Evangelical Theological Seminary, exhibited how similar the creedal positions of the two churches were.

Prior to the Uniting Conference, Professor Albert C. Outler wrote, at the request of the Joint Commission, a preface to Part II—Doctrinal Statements and the General Rules, which was important for those concerned about this issue. It follows:

The doctrinal traditions of both The Methodist Church and The Evangelical United Brethren Church stem from the Evangelical Revival of the 18th century and have been conserved and developed through the generations until now. In this Plan of Union it is proposed that this vital heritage be cherished and its authentic development insured.

In their original Constitution (1808) the American Methodists placed a Restrictive Rule designed to inhibit irresponsible doctrinal changes, "contrary to our present existing and established standards of doctrine." This Rule has remained in force and unamended through subsequent schisms and reunions. It was renewed by the Uniting Conference of 1939 and is once again repeated in the Plan of Union (Part I, Section III, paragraph 16).

The phrase, "our present existing and established standards of doctrine," has never been formally defined. In its original reference, however, it included as a minimum John Wesley's forty-four *Sermons on Several Occasions* and his *Explanatory Notes Upon the New Testament*. Their function as "standards" had already been defined by the "Large

Minutes" of 1763, which in turn had been approved by the American Methodists in 1773 and 1785. To the *Sermons* and *Notes* the Conference of 1808 added *The Articles of Religion*—an abridgement of the XXXIX Articles of the Church of England prepared by Mr. Wesley in his revised version of *The Book of Common Prayer* ("The Sunday Service").

In 1962 after sixteen years of union under two confessions of faith, The Evangelical United Brethren Church adopted a *Confession of Faith* based upon the doctrinal traditions of the former Church of the United Brethren in Christ and The Evangelical Church and intended as a covenient summary of the basic beliefs of evangelical Christianity. In the present Plan of Union, this *Confession* is placed alongside *The Articles of Religion* and becomes a stipulated reference in the Restrictive Rules. The *Confession, The Articles of Religion* and the Wesleyan "standards" are thus deemed congruent if not identical in their doctrinal perspectives and not in conflict.

The purpose of such standards is certainly not to displace the direct and primary authority of the Bible nor to stultify the responsible freedom of thoughtful Christians in the development of Christian doctrine. In all matters of faith and morals, the authority of Holy Scripture stands supreme (cf. Article V in *The Articles of Religion* and Article IV in the *Confession*). Moreover, in the ongoing enterprise of theological reflection, the Wesleyan "standards" had been rightly construed as the negative limits of public teaching in the church rather than the positive prescription of an inflexible system of doctrine. The principle was clearly stated in the *Deed of Union of the British Methodist Church* (1932):

> The *Notes on the New Testament* and the *Forty-Four Sermons* are not intended to impose a system of formal or speculative theology on Methodist Preachers, but to set up standards of preaching and belief which should insure loyalty to the fundamental truths of the Gospel of Redemption and insure the continued witness of the Church to the realities of the Christian experience of salvation.

Our concern is that those Wesleyan doctrinal traditions shall continue as a fruitful source of theological understanding. They make no pretension to infallibility in and of themselves. Mr. Wesley constantly appealed to Scripture as the primary locus of divine revelation and to the historic creeds and "the catholic spririt" as the larger context in which the Scriptures are to be interpreted. In like manner the Wesleyan "standards of doctrine" are designed to serve those who preach and teach in The United Methodist Church as sound guides to valid doctrine.[14]

This preface seemed to whet the appetite of the Uniting Conference for a fresh study of the creedal statements of the new church not so much for a new statement designed to replace the Confession and the Articles of Religion but much more to teach United Methodists how to *do* theology. Consequently, the Uniting Conference voted to create a Creedal Statement Study Commission and specified the composition of the commission.

The Creedal Statement Study Commission shall be composed of twenty-seven members elected by the Uniting Conference, upon nomination of the Council of Bishops, the membership to include: (a) seven selected from the faculties of the theological schools related to The United Methodist Church; (b) four from each of the five jurisdictions, which four shall include in each case two clergy, one of whom shall be a parish minister and two laymen; and (c) of the total twenty-seven members at least three shall be women.[15]

Dr. Albert Outler, professor of historical theology of Perkins School of Theology, was elected chairperson and the Reverend Robert Thornburg, parish minister of First United Methodist Church of Peoria, Illinois, was elected secretary of the commission. Six women, rather than the three specified in the legislation, were included in the membership of the commission.

Decision to Study the Social Principles

Just as the two churches brought two creedal statements, they brought two social principle statements to the union. All members of the Joint Commission of Union and all delegates to the Uniting Conference realized that this condition had to be altered. The preface to Part III of the Plan of Union stated the case clearly.

The Methodist Church and The Evangelical United Brethren Church, parties to the Plan of Union, have demonstrated a concern for social justice and have taken forthright positions on controversial issues involving Christian principles. John Wesley's opposition to the slave trade and to smuggling was an early expression of work for social justice. Involvement in struggle for social justice has become an increasingly important part of the Wesleyan tradition.

The Methodist *Social Creed* and The Evangelical United Brethren *Basic Beliefs Regarding Social Issues and Moral Standards* are in agreement basically. The differences are largely in phraseology or emphasis.

The Methodist Social Creed was adopted in 1908 by the General Conference of The Methodist Episcopal Church (North) meeting in Baltimore. It was a prophetic landmark in the enunciation of Christian conviction on economic issues. The same year the newly formed Federal Council of Churches voted to accept a statement, *The Social Ideals of the Churches,* based upon it. In 1914 The Methodist Episcopal Church (South) and in 1916 The Methodist Protestant Church adopted *Social Creeds.* The Uniting Conference of these three branches in 1939 adopted a *Social Creed.*

The Uniting Conference of the Church of the United Brethren in Christ and The Evangelical Church in 1946 endorsed a statement on social beliefs based on the positions of the two uniting churches on social issues, patterned after the statements of the Federal Council of Churches.

Social statements of both The Methodist Church and The Evangelical United Brethren Church have been reviewed and revised by successive General Conferences to take into account new and changing social conditions. Both churches have been responding to social changes and complexities by increasing involvement in research, education, and modes of action.

The Methodist *Social Creed* and the Evangelical United Brethren *Basic Beliefs Regarding Social Issues and Moral Standards* are important historical documents. The Plan of Union takes this into account by recording the text of each.[16]

The Uniting Conference elected a twenty-seven member commission to rewrite Social Principles for The United Methodist Church. Bishop James Thomas was elected chairperson. Mrs. Ted Baun of Fresno, California, was elected secretary.

Choice of a Quadrennial Emphasis

"A New Church for a New World" was the general theme chosen for the quadrennial emphasis, 1968–1972. The United Methodist Church was a new church and, in the light of change, the world is always somewhat new. The biblical text set over the theme was II Corinthians 5:17–18: "If any one is in Christ, he is a new creation; the old has passed away, behold, the new has come. All this is from God, who through Christ reconciled us to himself and gave us the ministry of reconciliation."

The stated purpose was the renewal of the church through three responses of significant witness: (1) the Church and the Word, (2) the Church and Its Work, and (3) the Church and the World.

The Church and the Word was an emphasis of specific study of the Sermon on the Mount. John Wesley once referred to the Sermon on the Mount as "the noblest compendium of religion to be found even in the oracles of God."

The Church and Its Work was explained in part as follows: "We recommend that the ministries on the local level be examined immediately to see whether they are relevant in today's world. We expect that each congregation will see itself as part of the church in process of renewal. An essential part of this renewal is leadership development of the laity in order that it may assume its full role in life and mission of the new church."

The Church and the World emphasized "the church's witness in the world is one of reconciling love. This means we must find effective ways to speak the Eternal Word—the Good News of Christ—so that it may be heard intelligently, believed gladly, obeyed willingly and received convincingly because it is backed by authentic action."

An important part of the quadrennial emphasis was the Fund for Reconciliation of $20 million to be raised over and above regular giving. Its purpose was "to engage in constructive social change relative to the church's mission in the world . . . such as reconstruction in war ravaged areas."

This decision for a quadrennial emphasis, "A New Church for a New World," may have been the most effective means employed by the Uniting Conference to address "the unfinished business of an unfinished church." Bishop James K. Mathews was chosen chairperson of a large committee to guide the emphasis.

A One-Day General Conference

The Enabling Legislation provided for a one-day General Conference at the conclusion of the Uniting Conference. Mr. Parlin explained the necessity of it this way: "There might be a quibble as to the authority of the Uniting Conference, but if we have the acts of the Uniting Conference now ratified and adopted by this, the official General Conference, there can be no doubt."

The names Charles C. Parlin and Paul A. Washburn have frequently appeared in this book. Perhaps it will not be outside of good taste to record here one portion of the record of that one-day General Conference that reveals the relationship that existed between us.

Charles Parlin: Mr. Chairman, before I introduce about five resolutions necessary to wind up our business, just a word of personal privilege. I think the circumstances have created an unfortunate and erroneous illusion. The work of the Joint Commission has been done by thirty-eight members, nineteen from each of the former denominations. They met and delegated a great deal to the executive committee of fourteen. When they met and came to an impasse and a difficult decision, a hard decision, it was referred to the officers. Those officers were from the former Evangelical United Brethren Church: Bishop Mueller, Bishop Heininger, and Paul Washburn; and from the former Methodist Church: Bishop Wicke, Bishop Ensley, and myself. When the officers met, as we did quite frequently, and we had a difficult problem, it was often assigned to the two secretaries. Between us there was a very unfair division of labor, because Paul Washburn was working on this job full-time and I was trying to carry on my law practice and do this. I think I spent approximately half my working time since Chicago on this and half on my own profession, but Paul has done full-time. His office was the clearing house; all the documents were prepared in his office in Dayton and I flew often to Dayton for conversation with him. By the rules of our Methodist Church, now adopted by The United Methodist Church, we silence all bishops, and you will note that of the officers Bishop Mueller, Bishop Heininger, Bishop Wicke, Bishop Ensley, and then after we got to Dallas, we silenced Washburn; I am the only man who can speak. I would just like to destroy the illusion that I have done all the work by calling to the microphone and asking for a privilege of a few words from the man who really did the work, my pal, Paul Washburn, now Bishop Washburn; I would ask the privilege of him saying a few words.

Bishop Paul Washburn: Months ago we could characterize our spirit by saying, "And I saw a new heaven and a new earth." I trust that we do not now assume that we have arrived. We have work to do and miles of the spirit to go before we have arrived at the one church of Jesus Christ which the times demand. In this spirit, Dr. Parlin and I have tried to do our work and we do rejoice with the rest of you in the kind of celebration we have had here. It has not been a celebration of doxologies only, but a celebration of a people who know that it is our life to try and do our faith. This for me has been the concept of dedication which has characterized this Conference and I am grateful for what I have beheld here. All of you know that Dr. Parlin is a lawyer and that I am just a mine-run preacher, but we have had a rather consistent experience as we've traveled about together, illustrated in what happened in Minot, North Dakota. We were on a platform where there were antagonistic Evangelical United Brethren and antagonistic Methodists, but the majority of those present were with us. All the questions that dealt with doctrine were directed to Dr. Parlin and all the questions that dealt with law were directed to me. This has been the character of our life together and I think we ought to shake hands at the end of this affair.[17]

Mr. Parlin died in mid-November of 1981, a layman who had exhibited uncommon loyalty to the church of his choice but also to the church of Jesus Christ in all the world. He served terms as the president of the World Council of Churches and of the World Methodist Council. He served faithfully in his local church in Englewood, New Jersey. He cared about the church's oneness in every place in each place. He dedicated his skills as a gifted lawyer to the task of helping to create the Plan of Union. He was my colleague, my mentor, and my friend. The United Methodist Church is, in large measure, a consequence of his skill as a designer of documents and an arbitrator of difficult issues.

Bishop W. C. Martin, veteran ecumenist, voiced the prayer with which the Dallas Conference ended. He prayed:

And now, Our Father, as we go, we thank Thee for the song of rejoicing in our hearts, for the conviction deep within us that, in spite of all its shortcomings due to human limitations and human frailities, this uniting, renewing Conference has begun, continued, and ended in Thee. We would pray above everything else that the loftiest dreams, the most daring hopes, the noblest ambitions and aspirations which we have experienced here may not fade or grow dim as we leave, but may become brighter and stronger, may there be renewed commitment as we go from this Conference to the places where the high plans of wider and richer ministry to human need in this land and in other lands which have been designed and approved by this Conference may be carried to their largest fulfillment. Give us journeying mercies, we pray Thee, as we leave this place. Bring us safely to our homes, whether near at hand or in the far places of the earth, and may the fellowship begun and renewed here never, never end. Be Thou with us until we meet again in another General Conference or that city not made with hands that cometh down from heaven. And now unto Him who is able to do exceedingly abundantly above all that we ask or think according to the power that worketh in us, unto Him be glory in the Church through Christ Jesus unto all generations, for ever and ever. Amen.[18]

11

Union Outside the United States

The union forming The United Methodist Church in 1968 influenced conferences and congregations of the uniting churches outside the United States in several ways. In Japan both churches had entered the Church of Christ in Japan at the time of World War II and had continued to support mission projects and missionaries there. In the Philippine Islands, the Evangelical United Brethren Church had entered the United Church of Christ in the Philippines. The Methodist Church had not. The Philippines Central Conference of the Methodist Church embraced five Annual Conferences there. These facts illustrate the multiple kinds of relationships The United Methodist Church had with churches outside the United States of America. The impact of the 1968 union was felt more keenly in Canada, the German Democratic Republic, the Federal Republic of Germany, and Switzerland.

Union in Canada

When the Methodist Episcopal Church was born at the Christmas Conference of 1784, that church expressed mission by setting apart Freeborn Garretson and James O. Cromwell for missionary service in Nova Scotia. They arrived in Nova Scotia early in 1785. By 1787, 426 members had been gathered into the Halifax Circuit. Garretson served there for only a brief period. Later he became presiding elder of the New York District and sent two young preachers, William Loose and David Kendall, to the Lake Champlain Circuit with instructions "to range at large in Canada."

Together they initiated the Methodist Mission in Upper Canada. This mission found an open door to Methodists on account of the zeal and energy of Philip Embury's widow, her second husband and her son, and Barbara and Paul Heck, who had emigrated to Canada because they were British loyalists.[1]

The work of The Methodist Episcopal Church prospered more in Upper Canada than in Nova Scotia. Missionaries who worked in Upper Canada included in addition to Loose and Kendall: Elijah Woolsey, James Coleman, Hezekiah Calvin Wooster, Samuel Coate, Nathan Bangs, William Case, and Henry Ryan. For a time, it appeared that the Upper Canada Mission would became "a large and prosperous division of The Methodist Episcopal Church." The progress was soon to be halted.

It was halted by war. Patriotism proved stronger than religion. The second war between the United States and Great Britain (1812–14) made American missionaries insufferable in Canada. Though it took more than a decade to settle affairs, the bond of union among Methodists in the two countries was officially severed, and in October, 1828, the American Methodist mission was transformed into The Methodist Episcopal Church of Canada. Really, the Americans had given up four years earlier, and after thirty-three years of heroic evangelism had created an Annual Conference of 2 districts, 21 circuits and missions, 36 preachers, and 6,150 members.[2]

It is important to note that the Methodist Episcopal Church of Canada prospered and became one of the strongest Protestant churches there. In 1925 it participated in the formation of the United Church of Canada.

The Church of the United Brethren in Christ entered into missionary endeavor in Canada in 1853 under the leadership of Israel Sloane. Mr. Sloane's work proved very successful and three years later had grown so that Bishop Glossbrenner organized the Ontario Conference with six itinerant ministers and over 150 members. This conference existed until 1905 when it united with the Congregational Church. At the time of that union, there were twenty-seven congregations with 1,453 members. It is important to note that the Congregational Church was another participant in the formation of the United Church of Canada.

The Evangelical Association appeared in Canada because, following the Revolutionary War and through the War of 1812, several German families moved from Pennsylvania to the Province of Ontario. In 1838 the first Missionary Society of the Evangelical Association was formed and determined to establish four missions. Two of these were the Waterloo and the Black Creek Mission-in Canada. Raymond Albright wrote in his *History of the Evangelical Church:*

In most respects the problems of The Evangelical Church in Canada have been the same as the problems of the church in the United States. Almost all of the churches in the eastern province of the Dominion use either the English or French language almost exclusively. The churches of the northwestern provinces, with some notable exceptions, are still almost exclusively German. These are scattered over a vast area covering three provinces: Manitoba, Saskatchewan, and Alberta with beginnings in British Columbia. Many of the German group are pietists and lead a devout life. Due to the vast distance from Ontario and to the fact that many of the preachers were not able, on account of these distances, to attend the sessions of the annual conference, a new conference was formed in 1926 and called the Northwest Canada Conference. In

1940 this group had 23 ministers under appointment and 2,400 members. The Canada Conference had 38 ministers under appointment and 9,000 members.[3]

In 1925 the Methodist Episcopal Church of Canada, the Congregational Church, and the Presbyterian Church united to form the United Church of Canada. Overtures were made to the Evangelical Church to participate in the union. These overtures were received graciously and given sympathetic and prolonged discussion but were finally rejected.

When the formulation of The United Methodist Church loomed on the horizon, the Northwest Canada Conference opposed the union and was granted permission to become an independent church under the name "the Evangelical Church of Canada." The Canada Conference decided that the time had come for it to unite with the United Church of Canada.

The Chicago General Conference of the Evangelical United Brethren Church authorized the union of the Evangelical United Brethren Church (Canada Conference) with the United Church of Canada. Union was consummated at a ceremony in Zion Church, Kitchener, Ontario, on January 10, 1968. Bishop Reuben Mueller preached the sermon. Finally, there was union of Methodists and Evangelical United Brethren in Canada.

The delegates from the Canada Conference were invited to the Uniting Conference in Dallas even though they were by that time members of the United Church of Canada. The Reverend Emerson Hallman, who had been the conference superintendent of the Canada Conference, spoke words of farewell. He said:

We are here today as a delegation through the courtesy of The Evangelical United Brethren Church. We were released from membership here to become part of The United Church of Canada and this is our last session in this gathering here. We feel it is only right that we express appreciation for the many years of relationship.

First as The Evangelical Church and then as The Evangelical United Brethren Church, we have had happy associations over the years. Most of our ministers in Canada have been trained in our schools particularly North Central College and Evangelical Theological Seminary. Bishops of this denomination have served our conference over many years. The relationships have been most happy. As we come to the end of this journey together, which began way back in 1837, we want to express the deep appreciation of the people of the Canada Conference for these years of association together as part of our denomination.

As we move into new relationships, we are finding those relationships to be most cordial. Provisions of the Plan of Union have been gracious and generous. Our people are moving forward in a wonderful spirit. We look toward being a vital part of the Christian Church in our country. Again, as we say farewell in this session, it is with appreciation of the wonderful association we have enjoyed over the years. Our prayers will be with you as you enter into new relationship in The United Methodist Church.[4]

Union in Europe

At the time of union, the Methodist Church included three Central Conferences in Europe: the Central Conference of Central and Southern Europe, the German Central Conference, and the Northern Europe Central Conference. Methodist congregations in seventeen countries related to the Methodist Church through twenty Annual Conferences: ten in central and southern Europe, five in Germany, and five in northern Europe.

The Evangelical United Brethren Church had one Central Conference in Europe with congregations in four nations: the German Democratic Republic, the Federal Republic of Germany, France, and Switzerland. Work in Poland had been destroyed during World War II. Because the Evangelical United Brethren Church had no churches in the Scandinavian or Baltic states, the Central Conference of Northern Europe was not directly involved in negotiating the union in Europe. At several junctures in the process, however, that Central Conference showed avid interest in the process.

All four of the Central Conferences bridged the political gap between Communist and non-Communist states. This bridging was especially important between churches in the German Democratic Republic and the Federal Republic of German. Resourceful persons serving on the European Commission on Union found ways to work within the limitations imposed by this fact. Awareness of this resourcefulness having its roots in Christian convictions was verbalized in an address by the Reverend Herbert Eckstein, the chairman of the Evangelical United Brethren portion of the negotiating committee. Mr. Eckstein lived in West Berlin and his experiences there add profundity to his words:

The unity of the Church, given in Christ to the Church from the beginning and assigned to her, is according to his word under the promise of blessing. The riches of his giving he did not promise to large numbers or strong organizations, but to those who stand together for his work. This knowledge, and not political reasons, drives us together. The knowledge of our common heritage, our common confession of faith as well as our common mission, is the deepest reason for our church union. . . . Our common striving after a new unity wakes us up to consciousness, to rethinking, and for the gathering of all gifts and powers. The variety of the members of Christ's body is newly recognized and accepted. So union is not only a concentration of existing organizations and the heritage of both sides, it brings also a mutual completion and enrichment to the whole spiritual organism of the church.[5]

Another conviction of great importance to congregations and conferences in Communist and non-Communist countries guided the European Commission on Union. It was voiced in a report on negotiations given by the Reverend Hermann Jeuther, chairman of the Methodist Commission on Church Union in December, 1964. Mr. Jeuther said: "We deem it indispensable that our work in Europe should be coordinated with the work of the Commission on Church Union in the United States of America. We wish to emphasize that we have been one church until now (United States of America, Europe, etc.) and we want to be and remain one church after union.'[6]

The theological realism and the sense of cherished connectionalism expressed by Mr. Eckstein and Mr. Jeuther undergirded union negotiations but did not keep the commissioners from facing the multifaceted reasons favoring the union nor the difficult issues needing solution along the road to union.

In the same report mentioned above, Mr. Jeuther spoke of the elements of far-reaching agreement on the following points:

1. In the Confession of Faith and the Articles of Faith;
2. in the Constitution and characteristic features of the *Discipline;*
3. in the conception of membership and the structure of the local church;
4. in the conception of the ministry and the episcopacy;
5. in the ways of work in Quarterly, Annual, Central, and General Conferences;
6. in the order of temporal economy and the administration of landed property; and
7. in the work of Church Institutions: Seminaries, Publishing Houses, Deaconess Hospital and Homes, and Social Establishment.

These, then, were powerful motivating forces for union in Europe: the conviction that the unity of the church is a gift from Christ to his church that transcends political divisions; the desire to remain one with The United Methodist Church in all the world; the elements of far-reaching agreement; all of which had been obvious to the churches in Europe for many years. Bishop Hermann Sticher, in a paper entitled "The Union of the Evangelical and Methodist Churches," wrote in 1980, "This fundamental perspective however, did not cause the leaders to stray from common sense."[7]

Commissions on Union were appointed with equal representation from the Evangelical Church and the Methodist Church and eventually subcommissions were appointed in the German Democratic Republic, in the Federal Republic of Germany, and in Switzerland. The European commissions were careful about the maintenance of communication with the commission in the United States and the commissions in the three European nations.

In introducing his readers to the problems in the union, Bishop Sticher wrote:

Along with the strong motives behind the union were a number of problems. They were chiefly, as the union discussions quickly determined, of a theological/doctrinal nature, because the Evangelical Church was more Lutheran and reformed than Wesleyan. Above all, it was scarcely noticed that behind the commonly used words

many differing conceptions could be hidden. Definite differences in the understanding of "church" had developed and become reinforced over two hundred years of
work on the part of the separate churches. The Evangelicals understood themselves
more as a community, and Methodists considered themselves more of a church, a
world-wide church moreover. . . . Altogether, however, the work on the
foundations of theology received all too little attention. That was certainly due to the
fact that the organizational motives had taken precedence over the spiritual.[8]

The Name of the United Church

Evidence that the commission in Europe worked from both theological
and practical perspectives can be demonstrated by recording here Bishop
Sticher's discussion of the problem of taking a name for the church in Europe.

Superintendent G. Zaiser, the first Chairman of the Evangelical Union Committee,
wrote in his report to the Central Conference: "The name of the future united church
is of great importance in order to win our congregations and members to the union
with the Methodist Church." In 1943, in the context of previous discussions of
union, the name German Evangelical Free Church was in the fore. Names which now
were being discussed were Evangelical United Free Church, United Evangelical Free
Church, Evangelical Community Church and Evangelical Methodist Free Church, a
name which appeared in the second session of the Union Committee on September
6–7, 1963. Out of the proposed names, one problem quickly presented itself,
whether the united church wanted to take on the designation, Methodist. There was
some resistance, because the Evangelical representatives maintained that "Methodist" had the stronger connotation of a sect, than "Evangelical Church;" they also
feared that the Methodist would quickly dominate the church name. But the
conviction was soon realized that the designation "Methodist" historically and
ecumenically expressed the free church movement known to the entire world, and it
therefore could not be omitted from the new church name. The designation "free
church" was withdrawn, in order to avoid the danger of confusion with other names,
and also out of the consideration that "free church" could only be justified in the
context contrasted to the state of the national church. It was agreed that in the
naming of the church, the new name should indicate that both churches had their
roots in a common heritage and the unyielding goal of a united church. At the fourth
session of the Commission on Union on February 18–19, 1965 the name Evangelical
Methodist Church was decided upon. The decision was explained by Superintendent
Eckstein as follows. "The word **Evangelical** witnesses to the fact that the Gospel
stands as the sole foundation of our church life and actions . . . the connection with
the **Methodist** represents the character of the new church. The Geneva District of the
Switzerland Conference assumed this name for its German-speaking area. The usage
of the name Evangelical Methodist Church was ratified by the General Conference in
the United States and by the Central Conferences of Central and Southern Europe,
and of Germany. This name was effective as of June 1, 1968."[9]

Other Problems

Central Conferences in all of Europe gained permission to design and describe the Organization and Administration section of the *Discipline* in ways relevant to their regions. They also gained permission to elect Judicial Councils within their Central Conferences to deal with constitutional questions.

The location of a theological seminary in the German Democratic Republic was not a problem because the Evangelical Church and the Methodist Church had experienced joint efforts in theological education at Bad Klosterlausnitz since 1953. In the Federal Republic of Germany, the location of a theological seminary posed a more serious problem. The Methodists operated a seminary in Frankfurt am Main, and the Evangelicals operated another in Reutlingen. The Swiss ministerial students usually attended seminary either in Frankfurt or in Reutlingen. In resolution of this problem, the Central Conference decided to establish a united seminary as quickly as possible, approved academic departments, a curriculum, and fixed the number of faculty at six. Location was finally decided when the city of Frankfurt made decisions about road construction that isolated the seminary campus. The Frankfurt property was sold, and the expansion of the Reutlingen campus began immediately. The academic year began at the Reutlingen location on September 15, 1971.

Excellent cooperation had existed for a long time between the Methodist Anker Publishing Company in Frankfurt am Main and the Christian Publishing House of the Evangelical Church in Stuttgart. When Dr. Theophil Wendt, the director of the Anker Company, died suddenly in January of 1967, even before the decision on church union had been made, a joint committee on publishing houses elected Mr. H. Schafer, the director of the Christian Publishing House, as business director of the Anker Company and instructed him to unite both firms in Stuttgart by January 1, 1968.

Any discussion of union of the churches in Germany would be incomplete without reference to the church's social institutions. The Evangelical-Methodist Church in West Germany supports kindergartens, vacation homes, apartment houses for senior citizens, and homes for the elderly. There is also a strong deaconess movement. Within West Germany there are four deaconess mother-houses with 821 deaconesses and 13 hospitals. These hospitals provide 2,237 beds and are located in West Berlin, Frankfurt, Hamburg, Heidelberg, München, Nürnberg, Stuttgart, Ulm, Wiesbaden, and Wuppertal-Elberfeld.

The diaconal work of the Central Conference in the German Democratic Republic operates four hospitals: a gynecological hospital at Leipzig, a children's hospital at Halle, a surgical hospital at Plauen, and a rheumatic clinic at Karl-Marx-Stadt. The deaconesses and nurses for these hospitals are trained in the church's own nursing school at Leipzig. In addition to these institutions, there are four United Methodist homes for the aged and six youth camps run by The United Methodist Church.

Celebration of Union in Germany

With the union consummated in Dallas and with plans for union completed in the two Germanys, the Central Conference of Germany met in two sections to celebrate the union. The conference in the German Democratic Republic met in Dresden from May 18 to 22, and the conference in the Federal Republic of Germany met in Frankfurt am Main from May 25 to 30, 1968. Bishop Friedrich Wunderlich was assisted in leading the Dresden celebration by Bishop Franz Schafer of Switzerland. At Frankfurt, Bishops Friedrich Wunderlich and Reuben Mueller shared the task of presiding over the conference. Dr. Charles Parlin and Bishops Lloyd C. Wicke and Paul Washburn were in Frankfurt to participate in the celebration. Bishop Sticher describes the core of the event as follows:

Bishops Mueller and Wunderlich used the same words which had been used in Dallas a few weeks previously: "We now declare jointly that the arrangements for the union of the Evangelical Church and the Methodist Church has been done legally according to the Constitution and the Enabling Legislation and that therefore the Evangelical Church and the Methodist Church are henceforth one church with the name Evangelical-Methodist Church. "The chairpersons of the Union Commissions and the secretaries of the two previous Central Conferences, four pastors, four lay persons, two youth and two church school students spoke in succession and finally all members of the Central Conference and the assembled body spoke the words: "Lord of the Church, we are united in you, in your church, and from now on in the Evangelical-Methodist Church."[10]

Bishop Wunderlich had reached retirement age by the time of the Central Conferences in Dresden and Frankfurt. He had been an important link between Methodists in the East and West and had crossed the border many times, rendering distinguished service in both countries. Delegates to the Dresden section were not permitted to vote but submitted a written declaration supporting Dr. Carl Ernest Sommer, former director of the Methodist Seminary in Frankfurt am Main, as their choice for bishop, Dr. Sommer was elected and consecrated at a service in St. Peter's Church in Frankfurt on May 29, 1968.

Union in the German Democratic Republic

Superintendent J. Falk of the Evangelical Church and Superintendent J. Vogel of the Methodist Church were the principal negotiators of the plan of union in the German Democratic Republic. They worked in close cooperation with Herbert Eckstein and Hermann Jeuther.

In addition to the celebration of union in Dresden on May 19, 1968, several significant celebrations were held in local congregations. In some cities, congregations were united even prior to the official celebrations in May. These union took place in cities where both or one of the churches had only small congregations and in cities such as Erfurt, Rostock, Greifswald, Schwerin, and Brandenburg. Following union, congregations were united in Magdeburg, Cottbus, Dresden, and Meissen.

Rumblings were being heard in Dresden in May of 1968 that the civil government would like to see a Central Conference for the German Democratic Republic. Pointing to the fact that The United Methodist Church granted autonomy to the Methodist Church in Cuba, they asked, "If The Methodist Church in Cuba can be autonomous and elect a Cuban as bishop why can not the same arrangement be made for the German Democratic Republic?" By 1790 a new Central Conference was formed there, and the Reverend Armin E. Härtel was elected to the episcopacy.

Dr. Rudiger Minor, professor at the theological school in Bad Klosterlausnitz, evaluated the union after twelve years, saying:

The United Church became one body, in the Annual Conference sessions; there is almost no difference between former Evangelical United Brethren and Methodist members. I consider it a great help for both churches, that by the union they became able to solve the problems which arose from the political situation in Germany. Within the framework of The United Methodist Church it is possible to be a relatively independent Central Conference with its own responsibility to fulfill its task in its situation. However, there was almost no awakening effect of the union. The loss of members was not stopped by the union.[11]

Union in Switzerland

Ten countries in which Methodist churches lived and worked were included in the Central Conference of Central and Southern Europe: Algeria, Austria, Belgium, Bulgaria, Czechoslovakia, Hungary, Yugoslavia, Poland, Switzerland, and Tunisia. Differences of cultures, languages, economic conditions, and political ideologies made this Central Conference one of the most difficult, if not *the* most difficult, to gather for meetings and to administer. Always some delegates were missing because they were not granted permission by their own governments to travel to the nation where the conference was in session. Differences in languages caused difficulties for presiding bishops, and in some countries bishops were not permitted to preside. William Nausner from Austria, writing in a pamphlet under the text, *Be eager to maintain the unity of the spirit through the bond of peace,* said:

The United Methodist Church confirms the Protestant idea of freedom for the individual; but this Church stands up at the same time for Christian unity.

But how is it possible to achieve unity and not oppress the individual at the same time? How is it possible to maintain freedom without giving up unity? According to Methodist Conviction the Christian answer is simply holiness! Because holiness is nothing else than perfect love, which "does not seek its own good, but the good of its neighbor." This love "binds everything together in perfect harmony." It is here where Methodism found its mission: "To spread holiness over the lands."

It is not really surprising that these continuing efforts have found an expression in the structure of The United Methodist Church. All of its history is marked by this struggle, to hold freedom and unity together through holiness. The Geneva Area is witness that this task is today as relevant as it has ever been.[12]

The Evangelical United Brethren Church had effective churches in France and Switzerland. They were connected to the whole church through membership in the Central Conference of Europe. Thus, union with the Methodist Church meant the addition of an eleventh nation, namely, France, to the Central Conference of Central and Southern Europe.

Bishop Sticher reports in his article on union:

On July 20, 1965, in Zurich, Bishop Reuben H. Mueller and Charles Parlin from the Commission on Union in the United States, Bishops F. Sigg and F. Wunderlich and Evangelical Superintendents D. Rosser and H. Eckstein and Methodist Superintendents F. Schwarz and F. Schafer participated in a dialogue, in which they came to a significant change of position: the unanimous decision that the Swiss Annual Conference of The Evangelical Church should become part of the Geneva district of The Methodist Church.[13]

Thus, Evangelical United Brethren—Methodist union further complicated an already complicated situation. At a conference in Strasbourg, France, Bishop Sigg described the complex situation as follows:

Much more than other episcopal areas in Europe we suffer through the fact that we do not have a consistent training for our ministers. In certain countries the training is too general, and perhaps additionally a little Methodism at the end. With the ten different languages no one can imagine a uniform literature or an effective news service. . . . Our church discipline is for a Methodist who holds a Church office, very often a secret book which can be used by just a few people. But a minimum of Church discipline for the local parish should exist in French, Flemish, Polish, Czechoslovakian, Hungarian and Serbian. . . . Each Church has something to give. Every Church is in need of something . . . this is an experience of the Geneva Area too. To discover the possibilities for exchange could be a fruitful task for the Central Conference. However, it is a joy to speak and the Geneva Area seeing it as a drill ground for the greatest task of Christianity: eager to maintain the unity of the Spirit in the Bond of Peace.[14]

The Strasbourg meeting of the Central Conference of Central and Southern Europe happened during a promising period of history for the ecumenical movement. "Within the Methodist Church the question of autonomy was under discussion and union with the Evangelical United Brethren was at hand. As a living sign of this coming union, Superintendent Daniel Roser from the Swiss Evangelical United Brethren Church was an official guest at this Central Conference."

One year later, Bishop Ferdinand Sigg died, leaving a vast void in the administration of the Geneva Area and in the plans for union. In September of 1966, Superintendent Franz Schafer was elected bishop of the Geneva Area.

Bishop Schafer explained the late date for the celebration in Berne by saying, "In Switzerland we wanted to complete the negotiations before we made decision to unite." So, from 1968 to 1969 there were two annual conferences in Switzerland: one former Evangelical United Brethren and the other former Methodist. Negotiations were carried forward by nine committees bearing the following names: 1—Discipline; 2—Church and Community; 3—Ministry; 4—Finance and Administration; 5—Community for Youth; 6—Community for Social Institutions; 7—Publishing House; 8—Foreign Missions and Women's Work (the Swiss had twenty missionaries at work elsewhere in the world); and 9—Choirs and Men's Work.

With negotiations completed, they were ready to celebrate. Four thousand members of the Uniting Conferences gathered in the Town Hall in the city of Berne. Ecumenical delegates were present from the Reformed Churches, the Roman Catholic Church, the Salvation Army, and the World Council of Churches. Bishop Eugene Frank represented the Council of Bishops, and Bishop Odd Hagen represented the Central Conference of Northern Europe.

The young people had built a wall as the center of attention in the hall and on the wall had erected a cross. Brass bands and choirs provided music for the event. Bishop Schafer preached from John 3:17: "For God sent the Son into the world, not to condemn the world, but that the world might be saved through him."

Bishop Schafer said in his Episcopal Message:

Because the Church is not called to propagate the American way of life, nor the European way of life, nor the way of life of any other nation, culture, or level of civilization; but is called rather to render a witness to Jesus Christ that is not limited in its vitality by national, regional, or local boundaries; we believe the world structure given in the order and tradition of our branch of The United Methodist Church should not be abandoned.[15]

Unifying forces can be seen best in situations where vast cleavages exist. Perhaps this fact accounts for the vitality of the Geneva Area. Bishop Sigg said it well:

In present history of Europe, in this highly important hour, there is no other Protestant Church more fitting of being a bridge builder, a mediator in reconciliation, a bearer of strong biblical convictions. The Geneva Area is situated on the crossroads between East and West, between Africa and Europe, between America and Russia; it has the duty to serve as an example of how churches can live together in the full sense of this word. The Geneva Area survived the catastrophe of the Second World War and shows to the entire church, that great differences within a church can be overcome, if the people have goodwill and if God is with them.[16]

Conclusions

Evangelical United Brethren and Methodist Churches in Europe faced formidable barriers to union. Three depths of experience seemed to have sustained them in their struggle for unity: (1) their struggle with current political ideologies; (2) their sense of belonging to a world church; and (3) their faith in a Lord who transcends and at the same time penetrates nations, cultures, and civilizations.

12

Penultimate Conclusions

With what realities shall we compare The United Methodist Church sixteen years after the union that brought it into being? Shall we compare The United Methodist Church to the Evangelical United Brethren Church as that church was before 1968? Or shall we compare The United Methodist Church to the Methodist Church as that church was before union? Following either of these paths will lead some with long memories—however faulty those memories may be—to some regrets and some gratifications. The United Methodist Church has expanded our horizons, multiplied our resources, enlarged our opportunities to minister, and called us to vital witnessing in the church and through the church to the world. But such nostalgic evaluation of The United Methodist Church is futile, for it is a fruitless search for what used to be—rich with memories but void of the pilgrimage toward the realm of God.

A more adequate way to evaluate The United Methodist Church is to compare her, her people, her congregations, her conferences, and her relationship to her world parish with New Testament images of the church like "the Body of Christ" or "the People of God."

A Theology of the Church

First Peter 2:10 provides an excellent standard against which to evaluate The United Methodist Church. It says, "Once you were no people but now you are God's people; once you had not received mercy but now you have received mercy." As Christian people within the whole people of God, we perceive that we have received mercy superlatively through the birth, growth, miracles, teachings, death, resurrection, and ascension of Jesus Christ—Jesus Christ who is God's living Word to us and who became flesh and dwells among us.

Christ's people of God are characterized by three conditions. The first of these is life in covenant with God in Christ and with God's people in Christ. Christians living in covenant have heard God's double promises, namely, "I will be your God" and "You will be my people." Grateful response to these promises moves the people of God to live out the love admonition (see Luke 10:27), to celebrate and nurture the corporateness of the church, and to work for the inclusiveness of the church. Galatians 3:26–29 describes that inclusiveness. It says, "In Christ Jesus you are all sons of God, through faith. For as many of you as were baptized into Christ have put on Christ. There is neither Jew nor Greek, there is neither slave nor free, there is neither male nor female; for you are all one in Christ Jesus. And if you are Christ's, then you are Abraham's offspring, heirs according to promise."

The second characteristic is life in pilgrimage. Many members of the church think of the church only as a sanctuary, a stronghold, a haven, a refuge in a time of trouble, and as such they want the church to be changeless, durable, and permanent. Sometimes the church is like this, but the people of God are always on the move from experience to experience, from day to day, from relationship to relationship, from week to week, from place to place, from year to year, and soon, from planet to planet. God's people are always on the way—always pilgrims—and there is no ultimate sanctuary save the sanctuary of the way.

A principle of alternation operates among God's pilgrim people. Sometimes they gather, and sometimes they scatter. They gather to be confronted by the living Word which is the living Christ, to celebrate the sacraments, and to be sent forth in mission. Christian pilgrims spend most of their time in secular settings where witnessing is expected. They ought always to exhibit that they are on their way from the new birth to the realm of God. Owning their pilgrim way causes fear of new experience, fear of change, fear of failure, fear of persecution, and fear of the future to be swallowed up in the security of the way.

The third characteristic of the people of God in Christ is servanthood. They possess and perfect their servanthood of remembering the servant Christ, by retelling stories about the servant Christ, by re-acting the servant Christ, and by re-presenting the servant Christ. They preach good news to the poor. They proclaim release to the captives. They bring sight to the blind. They heal the brokenhearted. They seek liberty for the oppressed, and they proclaim the acceptable year of the Lord. The time for their servanthood is now. The place for their servanthood is the place where they happen to be.

Living in covenant with God and God's people, taking pilgrimage from the new birth to the realm of God, and serving as Christ's ministers for Christ's sake reveal a rigorous biblical standard against which to evaluate the procedures and the consequences of the union that formed The United Methodist Church.

In this last chapter permit me to make a few brief observations, to celebrate the labors and the fruits of the labors of four postunion quadrennial commissions, and to ponder with my readers two questions: one about renewal in the church, the other about our unity in Christ. As we make our way through these observations, celebrations, and questions, let us be aware of the definition of the people of God described above.

Observation One

Too few women were involved in the work of the Joint Commission on Union. Prior to 1964, Helen C. Waters from Virginia was a member of the Methodist Commission on Union. Mrs. Porter C. Brown and Miss Theressa Hoover were members of the Ad Hoc Committee on Evangelical United Brethren union from 1964 to 1968. On the subcommittee of the Committee on the Board of Missions that negotiated legislation to guide the Women's Division were seven strong women: Mrs. Porter Brown, Miss Dorothy McConnell, Mrs. Glen E. Laskey, Miss Marion Baker, Mrs. Paul E. Horn, and Mrs. C. Newton Kidd. When Mrs. Laskey became ill, Mrs. A. B. (Myrta) Pfeiffer served as her proxy. From the time of the Chicago General Conference in 1966 until the Uniting Conference in 1968, Mrs. D. Dwight Grove served on the Evangelical United Brethren Commission.

Union negotiations reached their zenith in the committee working on the Women's Division of the Board of Missions and that committee suggested the name "United Methodist Women."

Documents on union might have been purged of sexist language and the entire plan might have been improved immeasurably if more women had been involved in the process. This observation questions The United Methodist Church about its intention to be a fully inclusive church.

The Uniting Conference broke with tradition and entered a new age when it elected Mrs. D. Dwight Grove to the Judicial Council. Mrs. Grove, who had served as the president of the Women's Society of World Service of the Evangelical United Brethren Church, was the first woman ever elected to the church's highest court.

Observation Two

Racial minorities, blacks, native Americans, Hispanics, and Asians were severely limited as participants in the union process. Prior to 1964, Bishop Matthew W. Clair, Jr., the Reverend Sumpter M. Riley, and Mrs. Helen C. Waters served on the Methodist Commission on Union. Sumpter M. Riley and Miss Theressa Hoover served on the Ad Hoc Committee from 1966 to 1968. There were no native Americans, no Hispanics, and no Asians involved in the negotiations.

Another commission, the Commission on Interjurisdictional Relations of the Methodist Church, worked on the elimination of the Central Jurisdiction over the same period of time that the Commission on Union worked at its appointed task. Surely, the elimination of the structures of segregation from the life of the church was as important as church union.

Once, before the Chicago Conferences, the officers of the Joint Commission on Union met with the Committee of Five to discuss "Study

Documents on the Realignment of the Central Jurisdiction." The Committee of Five included Bishop James S. Thomas, Dr. W. Astor Kirk, Dr. John H. Graham, the Reverend John Hicks, and Attorney Richard C. Erwin. That meeting had a profound influence upon the Enabling Legislation and provided an opening for input from the members of the Central Jurisdiction. Important as that meeting was, it did not compensate for the absence of blacks, native Americans, Hispanics, and Asians in the membership of the Joint Commission. Again, these facts lift the question about our covenant to be an inclusive community of God's people.

Observation Three

When the gavel sounded marking the close of the Uniting Conference in Dallas, it marked at the same time the end of the Central Jurisdiction. This act meant that the major structure that prolonged segregation in the uniting churches was ended. It did not mean, however, as I have indicated previously, that racism, either personal or institutional, was ended in The United Methodist Church. Now, sixteen years later, our church still needs the diligent efforts of her members and the vigilance of the Commission on Religion and Race to help us to be purged of the scourge of racism. Continued diligent effort is essential if we are to make our pilgrim way to a people in just covenant with one another.

Observation Four

At no time during the transition from two churches to one church was either of the churches or the united church without Constitutional Law or a *Book of Discipline*. These documents were not designed as restraints or as burdensome rules to guide the members and officials of the church. They constitute covenants entered into a fully democratic way. As such, they describe our corporate intentions about our identity as Christians, our style of life together, and the ways we will be servants of the world. The late Bishop Gerald H. Kennedy wrote in an introduction to *The Discipline of The Methodist Church (1960):*

The *Discipline* became a record of the successive stages of spiritual insight attained by Methodists under the grace of Christ. We have therefore expected that the *Discipline* would be administered, not merely as a legal document, but as a revelation of the Holy Spirit working in and through our people. We reverently insist that a fundamental aim of Methodism is to make her organization an instrument for the development of spiritual life. We do not regard the machinery as sacred in itself, but we do regard as very sacred the souls for whom the church lives and works. We do now express the faith and hope that the prayerful observance of the spiritual intent of the *Discipline* may be to the people called Methodists a veritable means of grace.[1]

Observation Five

The ministries of the general boards and agencies, their fundamental reasons for being, continued uninterrupted throughout the entire process of union. To be sure, wrinkles appeared in the cloth of structure and in the cloth of procedure, but the ministries suffered little because of the wrinkles. We do well to ponder what would have happened if one month's church school literature had failed to appear because of the union or if one patient in a mission hospital had been neglected for the same reason. Celebrate a relatively smooth transition! Servanthood continued without interruption.

Observation Six

Overlapping Annual Conferences were granted twelve years in which they could negotiate plans for union of such conferences. Commissioners feared that budgetary imbalances, differences in ministerial pensions, and methods for choosing conference or district superintendents might call for extensive negotiations in several areas of the church. By 1972, however, just four years after union, the work of uniting former Evangelical United Brethren and Methodist Annual Conferences was completed. In place after place, new Annual Conferences celebrated union and reiterated the words: "Lord of the church, we are one in thee, in thy church, and now in The United Methodist Church." There was almost a universal will to get on with the union of the church.

Observation Seven

The twelve-year rule guaranteed ratios of representation on the boards and agencies of the general church and in the delegations from Annual Conferences to General and Jurisdictional Conferences. Roughly speaking, the ratio was one former Evangelical United Brethren to seven former Methodists. The ratio of one to seven did not endow the smaller group with decision-making power in the councils of the church, but it did guarantee voice and vote in those councils. The minority group appreciated this feature of the Plan of Union.

Observation Eight

Underlying every effort of the Joint Commission was the attempt to distribute and balance the powers granted by the Constitution and the *Discipline* to legislative, executive, and judicial branches and to the general agencies of the church. This single intentionality of those persons who were at the heart of the movement toward union may account for the success of this union and may account for the failure of most of the previous attempts to bring these churches together. The distributing and balancing of power was essential to the regulation of our life together as covenant people.

Observation Nine

Sixteen years after union, many of our congregations and many of our members do not know, or do not seem to know, the name of our church. There has not been an Evangelical United Brethren Church nor a Methodist Church since April 23, 1968. It can hardly be expected where a former name is carved in stone that the name be changed, although in some places even that has happened. It can and ought to be expected, however, that on bulletin boards, on worship folders, and in speaking of our church we would call it by its proper name, "The United Methodist Church."

Observation Ten

Countless opportunities for new friendships, new relationships, and new opportunities to be in ministry have been afforded to members of our united church who have desired these experiences. I appreciated the words spoken to the Council of Bishops by Bishop James K. Mathews in 1978. He said:

Now we have completed ten years as The United Methodist Church and, of course, ten years as its Council of Bishops. We go back forty years as a Council of Bishops of The Methodist Church with a comparable Board of Bishops in The Evangelical United Brethren Church. As a united body we appear to have succeeded. Distinctions which may have characterized us as separate denominations appear largely to have been erased. There seems little reason to suppose that any stresses and strains we have experienced as a Protestant communion in the last decade would have been avoided in our previously separate state. The union has indeed gone well and the Council of Bishops has progressed.[2]

We have lived together for a seventh of a century in covenant, in pilgrimage, and in servanthood. We have wanted to be the people of God.

Work on Union Beyond 1968

Many delegates to the Uniting Conference, as well as many members of the Joint Commission on Union, identified areas of the plan where insufficient time had been spent in negotiation. Among these were Doctrinal Statements, Social Principles, Agency Structure, and General and District

Superintendency. The first three of these were addressed and provisions made for their revision during quadrennium 1968–1972, and the fourth was addressed and redefined during quadrennium 1972–1976. It is the labors and the fruits of the labors of these commissions working on union beyond union that we celebrate now.

Celebration One

There was a notion abroad that a new creed, done in more contemporary language, was essential to the formation of a new church. Persons holding this notion greatly overestimated the impact of the Confession (1962) on the life of the Evangelical United Brethren Church and greatly underestimated the direction the Theological Study Commission on Doctrine and Doctrinal Standards would take. Before presenting the report in 1972, Dr. Albert Outler introduced the members of the commission and said of them, "If you will wait until they are all standing, you may then express your thanks for a group of people who have worked as well and selflessly as I have ever had any opportunity to observe."

The report was in three parts: I—Historical Background, II—Landmark Documents, and III—Our Theological Task. In part one we find these words:

. . . there is a "marrow" of Christian truth that can be identified and that must be conserved. This living core, as our predecessors believed stands revealed in Scripture, illumined by tradition, vivified in personal experience, and confirmed by reason. Our forebears were very much aware, of course, that God's eternal Word never has been, nor can be, exhaustively expressed in any single form of words. They were also prepared, as a matter of course, to reaffirm the ancient creeds and confessions as valid summaries of Christian truth. But they were careful not to invest them with final authority or to set them apart as absolute standards for Doctrinal truth and error.[3]

There follows in part one of the report a carefully written history of Wesleyan Doctrinal Standards, the Articles of Religion (Methodist), and the Confession (Evangelical United Brethren). Discussing the fading force of doctrinal discipline, the report observes "it was the Wesleyan hymnody that served as the most important single means of communicating the doctrinal substance of the gospel and in its guardianship as well."[4]

And we dare not miss this point:

There are, however, at least two general principles with respect to the discipline of doctrine in The United Methodist Church on which there had been broad and basic agreement. In the first place, the *Articles* and the *Confession* are not to be regarded as positive juridical norms for doctrine, demanding unqualified assent on pain of excommunication. They are and ought to remain as important landmarks in our complex heritage and ought rightly to be retained in the *Discipline*.

There is likewise general agreement that The United Methodist Church stands urgently in need of doctrinal reinvigoration for the sake of authentic renewal, fruitful evangelism, and the effective discharge of our ecumenical commitments. Seen in this light, the recovery and updating of our distinctive doctrinal heritage—"truly catholic, truly evangelical and truly reformed"—takes on a high priority.[5]

Part two of the report presents the landmark documents: the Articles of Religion as reprinted from Wesley's original text in *The Sunday Service of the Methodists* (1784), the text of the Confession of Faith identical with that of its original in the *Discipline* of the Evangelical United Brethren Church (1969), and the General Rules of the Methodist Church.

Part three is entitled "Our Theological Task." The report indicates:

The purpose in Christian theologizing is to aid people who seek understanding of their faith, authentic worship and celebration, effective evangelical persuasion, openness to God's concern for the world's agony and turmoil, infusion of that faith in life and work, and courageous ministries in support of justice and love.[6]

The report declares these to be the distinctive emphases of United Methodists: God's endowment of each person with dignity and moral responsibility, the primacy of grace that is God's loving action in human existence through the ever-present agency of the Holy Spirit, an active stress on conversion and the new birth, the cherished conviction that faith and good works belong together, and the view of faith and its fruits issue in voluntary association and local initiative and to cooperation in an effective connectional polity.

The report goes on to ask: "By what methods can our doctrinal reflection and construction be most fruitful and fulfilling?"

The answer comes in terms of our free inquiry within the boundaries defined by four main sources and guidelines for Christian theology: Scripture, tradition, experience, reason.[7]

The concluding paragraph of the report of the Theological Study Commission on Doctrine and Doctrinal Standards deserves most to be celebrated:

As United Methodists see more clearly who we have been, as we understand more concretely what are the needs of the world, as we learn more effectively how to use our heritage and guidelines, we will become more and more able to fulfill our calling as a pilgrim people and discern who we may become. It is in this spirit that we seek to engage in the theological task with a confidence born of obedience, and we invite all our people to a continuing enterprise: to understand our faith in God's love, known in Jesus Christ, more and more profoundly, and to give this love more and more effective witness in word, mission and life.[8]

Our celebration of this report which became Part II of the *Discipline* (1972) ought to be permeated through and through with the awareness that we have witnessed the formation of another landmark document, destined to take its place with the other landmark documents of 1784 and 1962.

Celebration Two

A united church of the late twentieth century could not long tolerate two Statements of Social Principles: the Methodist Social Creed and Basic Beliefs regarding Social Issues and Moral Standards of the Evangelical United Brethren Church. Thus, the Uniting Conference elected a Social Principles Study Commission. Bishop James S. Thomas was elected chairperson of the commission.

Early in its work, the commission decided that a simple intermingling of the two former statements would not serve the church or the present age. Consultations were held in many sections of the church in an effort to discern what issues needed to be addressed. The final draft of Social Principles approved first by the commission and finally by the General Conference of 1972 can well be celebrated. Its preamble states:

We, the people called United Methodists, affirm our faith in God our Father, in Jesus Christ our Saviour, and in the Holy Spirit, our Guide and Guard.

We acknowledge our complete dependence upon God in birth, in life, in death, and in life eternal. Secure in his love, we affirm the goodness of life and confess our many sins against his will for us as we find it in Jesus Christ. We have not always been faithful stewards of all that has been committed to us by God the Creator. We have been reluctant followers of Jesus Christ in his mission to bring all persons into a fellowship of love. Though called by the Holy Spirit to become new creatures in Christ, we have resisted the further call to become the people of God in our dealings with each other and the earth on which we live.

Grateful to God for his forgiving love, in which we live and by which we are judged, and affirming our belief in the inestimable worth of each individual, we renew our commitment to become faithful witnesses to the gospel, not alone to the ends of the earth, but also to the depths of our common life and work.[9]

Who does not celebrate the fact that our Social Principles are set in a context of doctrinal understanding and spirited devotion? The Reverend Melvin Talbert, in introductory remarks about the report of the commission, said, "The theme for our document is community. This concept became an exciting one for us. When we recognize that it is within the various communities that we find ourselves and are challenged to work out our existence."[10] The statement goes on to describe the communities in which we exist and to describe adjustments we make to those communities because we want to express our faith in action. The communities are: the natural world, the nurturing community, the social community, the economic community, the political community, and the world community. Under these headings our Social Principles are classified and set forth in clarity. Finally, the commission provided a new Social Creed:

We believe in God, Creator of the world; and in Jesus Christ, the Redeemer of creation. We believe in the Holy Spirit, through whom we acknowledge God's gifts, and repent our sin in misusing these gifts to idolatrous ends.

We affirm the natural world as God's handiwork and dedicate ourselves to its preservation, enhancement, and faithful use by humankind.

We joyfully receive, for ourselves and others, the blessings of community, marriage, sexuality and the family.

We commit ourselves to the rights of men, women, children, youth, and the aging; to improvement of the quality of life; and to the rights and dignity of ethnic and religious minorities.

We believe in the right and duty of persons to work for the good of themselves and others, and in the protection of their welfare in so doing; in the rights to property as a trust from God, collective bargaining, and responsible consumption; and in the elimination of economic and social distress.

We dedicate ourselves to peace throughout the world and to the rule of justice and law among nations.

We believe in the present and final triumph of God's Word in human affairs and gladly accept his commission to manifest the life of the gospel in the world. Amen.[11]

It is doubtful that a new Social Principles Statement would have been forthcoming except as an adjunct to the union. And what an excellent statement it is and worthy of study and acceptance by United Methodists everywhere. One of the best ways to celebrate this gift is to seek to live out its declarations. Surely every congregation in the connection could periodically make liturgical use of the Social Creed to the edification of the faithful.

Celebration Three

Comments about the organizational structure of boards and agencies of the church ran from "cumbersome" to "grown up like Topsy" to "lacking flexibility" to "too much bureaucracy" to "too much concentrated power." Sentiments such as these prompted the Uniting Conference to elect a Structure Study Commission. The commission elected Dr. Dow Kirkpatrick as its chairperson and Dr. Joel McDavid as its secretary. Hearings were held in many areas of the country in order to hear what members were saying about the board structure.

In reporting to the General Conference in 1972, Dr. Kirkpatrick said:

What we have heard in these four years from the church at all levels clearly is that the elements in the Board and Agency structures of The United Methodist Church which offer the least power for mission in the future and maybe even some drag are those elements which cannot be dealt with by amending one board here and another one there. Rather, these elements are part of the whole system and they must be dealt with in their wholeness if this system is to be renewed.

The twinful side of this system is first, that General Agencies resource the local church in its mission and, secondly, that the General Agencies make possible mission-fulfillment by doing those things on behalf of local disciples that can only be done by being together as a corporate entity. The criteria for judging our model, by which we judge it ourselves, are coordination, ongoing accountability, flexibility within this accountability, the representation of the pluralities of the church, and the kind of effectiveness which comes from efficiency and economy.[12]

The chief gift of the Commission on Structure to the church was a strengthened General Council on Ministries. Dr. Richard Cain said in presentation of the council:

It is the hope of the Structure Commission in proposing the Council on Ministries (replacing the General Program Council) that we are following very carefully the time-honored and well-proven principle of our church life, that the Annual Conference shall be present by its representative whenever there are key decisions to be made in the life of the church. You will note that the Council on Ministries has as its basic membership those who are elected in a free election by the Annual Conference, the fundamental body.

It would appear that the primary power entrusted to the Council on Ministries is that they will be in continual review and have authority to act with reference to structure in the life of the church after it has been recommended by the stated Boards and subject to the subsequent ratification of each General Conference, but it does provide flexibility.[13]

An additional part of the report spoke of the foci upon which the sights of four boards, suggested by the report, were fixed:

The Board of Church and Society is an attempt to focus the attention of the church upon the social issues of our time.

The Board of Discipleship is an attempt to focus the energies of the general church upon the needs of the local church.

The Board of Global Ministries is an attempt to focus the interest of the general church upon global consideration, that is, what does the gospel of Christ have to say on six continents.

The Board of Higher Education and Ministry is an attempt to focus the mind of the church upon the preparation of personnel for the ongoing life and work of the church.[14]

Celebration of the work of the Commission on Structure has taken the forms of negation, apathy, and affirmation. Each new General Conference seems to think that it can do a better job of structuring the general agencies. Each new attempt becomes costly and hinders the flow of mission intentionality of the local churches because the general agencies exist to be clear channels of mission resources from their point of origin to their destination. It is clear that this celebration is strained between the no and the yes.

Celebration Four

From the very beginning of the Methodist Episcopal Church, questions about the episcopacy have been raised. John Wesley questioned Francis Asbury and Thomas Coke as to why they took to themselves the title of bishop. For several decades various sections of the church debated the power of bishops over against the power of the General Conference. In these latter times, questions have been raised about the appointive power of bishops and tenure for bishops. The event of union in 1968 lifted sharply the question of life episcopacy versus term episcopacy, and the trends of the times toward self-determination sharpened the questions of appointive power. It was not until 1972 that a Commission to Study Superintendency was elected, but it is fair to assume that the election of the commission was inspired by questions about the episcopacy that were being asked at the time of union.

The commission, under the leadership of Dr. Merlyn Northfelt, did one of the most thorough studies of superintendency that has been done in modern times. They finally opted for life tenure for bishops and promoted legislation that holds bishops and district superintendents responsible for consultation with pastors and Pastor-Parish Relations Committees in making appointments. The decisions of the commission, and ultimately the decision of the General Conference, were grounded in the following theological understanding of the church and its mission:

The task of superintending in The United Methodist Church resides in the office of bishop and extends to the district superintendent, with each possessing distinct responsibilities. From apostolic times, certain ordained persons have been entrusted with the particular task of superintending. Those who superintend carry primary responsibility for ordering the life of the Church. It is their task to enable the gathered Church to worship and to evangelize faithfully.

It is also their task to facilitate the initiation of structures and strategies for the equipping of Christian people for service in the Church and in the world in the name of Jesus Christ and to help extend the service in mission. It is their task, as well, to see that all matters, temporal and spiritual, are administered in a manner which acknowledges the ways and the insights of the world critically and with understanding while remaining cognizant of and faithful to the mandate of the Church. The formal leadership in The United Methodist Church, located in these superintending offices, is an integral part of the system of an itinerant ministry.[15]

Fine as this theological grounding of the role of general and district superintendents is, there are those members in the Council of Bishops who prefer to think of themselves also as pastors, teachers, and liturgical officers. The report of the commission pointed to these other roles of bishops, but that section of the report did not become part of the *Discipline*. That section says:

Clarification of roles and functions, especially as these arise out of ordination, is important to enable bishops and superintendents to be effective leaders. Three categories were used for analysis of the functioning of leaders: leaders performing by being, by saying, and by doing. These functions point to the roles around which the church has constructed expectancies: Word, sacrament and order.

a) Being Related to Sacrament—The category of "being" includes public roles such as celebrant, ordainer, spiritual leader, exemplar, and representative person—as well as actions or activities more personal, such as being a "holy person," a counselor, and a friend. In these ways, leaders fulfill the ministry of sacrament.

b) Saying Related to Word—The category of "saying" embraces first the bold proclamation of the Word. But it also includes speaking through appointment—making, presiding, judging, as well as defending the faith, taking a stance, and designing strategy. Thus leaders fulfill the ministry of Word.

c) Doing Related to Order—The category of "doing" including actions such as administering, enabling, and evangelizing, with a goal of transforming the world. These are carried on also while performing the duties of a superintendent, connectional officer, and corporate executive. Thus, leaders fulfill the ministry of order.[16]

Such insights into the nature and role of the episcopacy are worthy of celebration and of gratitude to the commissioners who made the study and shepherded their findings through the chief legislature of the church.

The ten observations made and the four celebrations suggested reveal that United Methodists are caught between the church as the people of God on the one hand and the church as an institution on the other. A wedding of these ways of perceiving the church in one person, in one congregation, or in one conference seems difficult to achieve. Emphasis on the church as institution can lead to tinkering with the machinery of the church. It can also lead to improvement of the channels of ministry and mission. Emphasis on the church as the people of God can lead to romanticizing about the church. It can also lead to biblically justified being and action. In the observations made and in the celebrations suggested, there is evidence of United Methodists struggling to be the people of God living in covenant, in pilgrimage, and in servanthood while affirming the inescapable presence of an elaborate institution. What further proof is needed of the fact that The United Methodist Church is "An Unfinished Church"? But is not that unfinished state the prelude to growth in grace, to going on to perfection, and to the ultimate rule and realm of God?

Question One

Did the union of 1968 that brought The United Methodist Church into being bring with it any measure of renewal? Surely God is at work through the Holy Spirit trying to renew the church, and surely The United Methodist Church is one of the arenas in which God is at work. But are United Methodist persons, congregations, caucuses, and conferences communicating renewal in the Spirit to one another? Union provided means for such communication.

The union provided new and different associates to many persons. What was the nature of meetings between new associates? Did indifference mark the meetings? Did such persons meeting size up their new associates to determine their usefulness in furthering personal ambitions? Did the new associates find common grounds for the forming of lasting friendships? Did persons in such meetings find the presence of the living Christ in one another? Other types of meetings could be described, but perhaps it is already clear that the nature of meetings between new associates quantifies the measure of renewal attending the union. The gift of new associates was and is one of the factors offering renewal to the church.

The union provided new opportunities to exercise Christian disciplines over the substance of communications. The first Christians were given to telling and retelling stories about Jesus. They gossiped the gospel for a long time before they put it into writing. Since union, numerous opportunities have been afforded for disciplined communication of the good news: preaching clinics, choir schools, Bible studies, celebrations of the sacraments, and calls to participate in deeds of justice, peace, love, and joy. The quality of the communication quantifies the measure of renewal attending the union.

The union provided new corporate relationships. Opportunities to enter into covenants were greatly expanded. Opportunities to join other pilgrims on their pilgrim ways were multiplied. Opportunities to serve were enhanced. Connectionalism was quickened. To the extent that United Methodists appreciated and employed that new corporateness for mission, the church was renewed.

New dimensions of mission-oriented ministry were given to us. Dr. Herbert Eckstein of Berlin, West Germany, wrote of this opportunity for renewal, saying,

. . . every member of the new church is called by his readiness. Especially those who suffer under the spiritual poverty of the church should be ready to recognize and use God's new hour. All objections and fears must be set aside if nothing is to stop us on our new and common way. Out of faith in our Lord Jesus Christ and in our brothers and sisters we must produce courage for new ways, new changes, new efforts in mission.[17]

God is eternally ready to renew the church through the work of the Holy Spirit. What the church needs is a new sense of realism about the means of accepting renewal: the importance of new associates, the importance of disciplined communication of the good news, and the importance and power of proffered corporateness. As long as there are opportunities for growth in the use of these means of renewal in The United Methodist Church, that church is yet "An Unfinished Church."

Question Two

Did the united church receive, in any measure, Christ's gift of unity?

There can be little doubt that The United Methodist Church experienced institutional unity, and there can be little doubt that it experienced some measure of unity in Christ. But, at the same time, we cannot claim complete unity in Christ; our sinfulness prevents that and our denominationalism prevents that. When Jesus prayed "that they all may be one," his "all" referred to the whole company of the faithful, and The United Methodist Church is hardly the whole company of the faithful.

The unity for which Jesus prayed and the unity which we seek is unity in Christ. He is the wellspring of true Christian unity. When we receive Christ as our unity, we are bound together not by any single approach to the Scriptures but in him. When we receive Christ as our unity, we are bound together not by any system of doctrine but in him. When we receive Christ as our unity, we are bound together not by any method of evangelism but by the Evangel. When we receive Christ as our unity, we are bound together not by any form of servanthood, but simply by being servants of the world's people and systems in the name of Christ. When we receive Christ as our unity, we are bound together not by any parochial Christ but by the cosmic Christ. When we receive Christ as our unity, we are bound together not only by the Christ whom we understand but by the Christ who is yet partly mystery to us. Surely, there are living saints in The United Methodist Church who have found their unity, one with the other, and with the world's travail in Christ. Yes, the united church has, in many a measure, received the gift of unity but desires that gift the more.

Conclusion

On May 6, 1968, when the Uniting Conference that brought The United Methodist Church into being adjourned, that new church was an unfinished church. That church had new convenants to keep with God, with societies and persons within its own body, with Christians in other communities of faith, and with a salvation-hungry world which would require all of the foreseeable future for their fulfillment. That church had barely begun its faith pilgrimage into the final quarter of the twentieth century. That church was set in a world of persons and systems that cried bitterly for Christian service. A church faced with starving persons, naked persons, homeless persons, nationless persons, jobless persons, justiceless persons, and peaceless persons is by definition unfinished because its work is not done.

And who would have dared to say of that May day in 1968 that The United Methodist Church was truly catholic, truly evangelical, or truly reformed? If the church understands its reformation as an ongoing process that will continue until the end of time, members of the church should quickly claim their unfinished condition.

Now, sixteen years later, The United Methodist Church is still unfinished, and fortunate indeed are these United Methodists who know that their church is unfinished and who see "an unfinished church" as an opportunity to go on to perfection.

Notes

1. Celebration of Union

1. *Daily Christian Advocate,* April 25, 1968, p. 133.
2. Ibid., p. 133.
3. Ibid., p. 134.
4. Ibid.
5. Ibid., p. 135.
6. Ibid.
7. *Journal* of 1968 General Conference, p. 360.

2. Rootage in the Reformation

1. Harry Emerson Fosdick, *Great Voices of the Reformation* (New York: Random House, 1952), p. 92.
2. Ibid., p. 91.
3. Ibid., p. 81.
4. Williston Walker, *History of the Christian Churches,* ed. Robert T. Handy (New York: Scribner; 1959), p. 345.
5. Fosdick, Luther's "Address to the Christian Nobility of the German Nation," in *Great Voices of the Reformation,* pp. 97–98.
6. Walker, *History of the Christian Church,* p. 360.
7. Fosdick, Zwingli's "First Helvetic Confession," in *Great Voices of the Reformation,* p. 157.
8. Fosdick, Zwingli's "Account of the Faith," in *Great Voices of the Reformation,* p. 183.
9. Ibid., p. 189.
10. Walker, *History of the Christian Church,* p. 363.
11. Ibid., pp. 393–94.
12. Ibid., p. 455.
13. A. James Armstrong, *United Methodist Primer* (Tidings, 1972), p. 12.
14. T. Otto Nall, *By John Wesley* (New York: Association Press, 1961), pp. 15–16.
15. Paul W. Milhouse, *Philip William Otterbein* (Nashville: The Upper Room, 1968), p. 17.
16. Paul Blankenship, "History of Negotiations for Union between Methodists and non-Methodists in the United States" (diss.), p. 177.

17. Paul W. Milhouse, *Theological and Historical Roots of United Methodists* (Cowan Printing and Lithograph Company, 1980), p. 84.

18. Emory Stevens Bucke, *The History of American Methodism,* Vol. 1 (Nashville: Abingdon Press, 1964), p. 41.

19. Arthur Core, *Philip William Otterbein—Pastor Ecumenist* (United Brethren Printing Establishment, 1860), pp. 123, 129.

3. Early Relationships

1. John Lawrence, *United Brethren Church History* (United Brethren Printing Establishment, 1860), pp. 128-29.

2. Ibid., p. 124.

3. Henry Spayth, *History of the Church of the United Brethren in Christ* (United Brethren Printing Establishment, 1850), p. 20.

4. Lawrence, *United Brethren Church History,* p. 130.

5. Ibid., pp. 137–38.

6. Raymond W. Albright, *A History of the Evangelical Church* (Harrisburg, Pa.: The Evangelical Press, 1942), pp. 24–25.

7. Ibid., pp. 25–26.

8. Ibid., pp. 30–31.

9. Ibid., pp. 31–32.

10. Ibid., p. 35.

11. Bucke, *History of American Methodism,* vol. 1, p. 98.

12. Ibid., p. 98.

13. Ibid., p. 99.

14. Albright, *History of the Evangelical Church,* pp. 59–60.

15. Lawrence, *United Brethren Church History,* p. 218.

16. Bucke, *History of American Methodism,* vol. 1, p. 95.

17. Lawrence, *United Brethren Church History,* p. 219.

18. Albright, *History of the Evangelical Church,* p. 69.

19. Lawrence, *United Brethren Church History,* p. 344.

20. Ibid., pp. 366–67.

21. Albright, *History of the Evangelical Church,* p. 185.

4. Experience with Rifts and Reunions

1. Daniel Berger, *History of the Church of the United Brethren in Christ* (United Brethren Publishing House, 1897), p. 354.

2. Albright, *History of the Evangelical Church,* pp. 278–79.

3. Ibid., p. 333.

4. Ibid., p. 326–27.

5. Ibid., p. 328.

6. Ibid., p. 377.

7. Bucke, *History of American Methodism,* vol. 1, p. 603.
8. Ibid., p. 606.
9. Ibid., pp. 608–609.
10. Bucke, *History of American Methodism,* vol. 2, p. 287.
11. James H. Straughn, *Inside Methodist Union* (Nashville: The Methodist Publishing House, 1958), p. 33.
12. Ibid., p. 37.
13. Ibid., p. 39.
14. Ibid., pp. 40–41.
15. Ibid., p. 43.
16. Bucke, *History of American Methodism,* vol. 2, p. 85.
17. John M. Moore, *The Long Road to Methodist Union* (Nashville: Abingdon-Cokesbury Press, 1943), p. 26.
18. Ibid., p. 193.
19. Bucke, *History of American Methodism,* vol. 3, p. 444.
20. Ibid., p. 452.
21. K. James Stein, "Church Unity Movements in the Church of The United Brethren in Christ until 1946" (diss.), p. 233.
22. Paul H. Eller, *These Evangelical United Brethren,* (Dayton, Ohio: The Otterbein Press, 1957), p. 10.
23. Ibid., p. 9.

5. From Exploration to Negotiation

1. Blankenship, "History of Negotiations for Union," p. 288.
2. *Proceedings of The General Conference of The Evangelical United Brethren Church, 1958,* (Dayton, Ohio: The Otterbein Press, 1958), p. 316.
3. Ibid., pp. 480–81.
4. *Journal of the 1960 General Conference of the Methodist Church* (Nashville: The Methodist Publishing House, 1960), pp. 2001, 2004, 2006.
5. Ibid., p. 1580.
6. *Proceedings of The General Conference of The Evangelical United Brethren Church, 1962* (Dayton, Ohio: The Otterbein Press, 1962), p. 686.

6. A Plan for a New Church

1. *Minutes of the Joint Commission,* 19 September 1963, p. 52.
2. *Minutes of the Joint Commission,* March 23 1965, p. 163.
3. *Minutes of the Joint Commission,* 24 March 1965, p. 169.
4. *Minutes of the Joint Commission,* 8 September 1965, p. 192.
5. *Minutes of the Joint Commission,* 9 September 1965, p. 193.
6. *The Book of Discipline of The United Methodist Church—1968* (Nashville: The Methodist Publishing House, 1968), p. 21.

7. Ibid., p. 29.

8. Ibid., p. 17.

9. Ibid.

10. *Daily Christian Advocate—1964*, p. 393.

11. *Discipline of The Methodist Church—1964*, (Nashville: The Methodist Publishing House, 1964), p. 341.

12. *Discipline of The Evangelical United Brethren Church—1967* (The Board of Publication of The Evangelical United Brethren Church, 1967), p. 252.

13. *The Book of Discipline of The United Methodist Church—1968*, p. 363.

14. Curtis A. Chambers, "How Evangelical United Brethren Look at Methodist Union," *Central Christian Advocate*, 15 April 1966, pp. 145–47.

7. Contention over Union

1. *Minutes of the Joint Commission*, 10 September 1965, p. 207.

2. Evangelical United Brethren for Church Renewal, "Issues for A Union: A Biblical and Theological Perspective," p. 9.

3. Kenneth W. Copeland," Union as Methodists See It," an address to the Council of Bishops, 4 May 1966, p. 1.

4. James K. Mathews, *Resolution on Evangelical United Brethren and Methodist Union*, for the Commission on Ecumenical Affairs, 9 March 1966.

5. Lance Webb and Richard Cain, "Union Now or Later," *Together*, 15 June 1966.

8. The Chicago General Conference—1966

1. *Daily Christian Advocate—1966*, p. 5.

2. Ibid., pp. 5, 9.

3. *Proceedings of the 1966 General Conference of The Evangelical United Brethren Church*, pp. 331-32.

4. Ibid., p. 718.

5. Ibid.

6. Ibid., p. 372.

7. *Daily Christian Advocate—1966*, p. 97.

8. Ibid., pp. 98–99.

9. From Chicago 1966 to Dallas 1968

1. *The Book of Discipline of The United Methodist Church—1968*, p. 67.

2. Ibid., p. 341.

3. Reuben H. Mueller and Lloyd C. Wicke, *One Spirit* (The Women's Division of the Board of Missions of The Methodist Church).

4. Reuben H. Mueller and Lloyd C. Wicke, *Helps for Voting on Union* (The Joint Commissions on Union), p. 6.

5. Ibid., p. 8.

6. Paul Washburn, *Light on the Way* (The Evangelical United Brethren Commission on Union, 1 January 1967).

7. W. Maynard Sparks, *Report to the Annual Conferences of the Western Area of The Evangelical United Brethren Church,* May 1965, p. 6.

10. The Dallas Uniting Conference—1968

1. *Daily Christian Advocate—1968,* p. 105.

2. Ibid., p. 106.

3. Ibid., p. 38.

4. Ibid., p. 39.

5. Ibid., p. 51.

6. Ibid., p. 53.

7. Ibid., p. 41.

8. Ibid., p. 9.

9. Ibid., p. 10.

10. Ibid., pp. 25–26.

11. *The Book of Discipline of The United Methodist Church—1968,* pp. 101–103.

12. Ibid., p. 106.

13. Ibid., p. 107.

14. Ibid., pp. 35–37.

15. Ibid., pp. 455–56.

16. Ibid., pp. 52–53.

17. *Daily Christian Advocate—1968,* p. 800.

18. Ibid., p. 805.

11. Union Outside the United States

1. Bucke, *History of American Methodism,* vol. 3, p. 588.

2. Ibid., pp. 588–89.

3. Albright, *History of the Evangelical Church,* pp. 413–14.

4. *Daily Christian Advocate—1968,* p. 161.

5. Herbert Eckstein, "United Church, Renewed Church," from an address to the European Commission on Union, pp. 2–3.

6. Hermann Jeuther, *Report to the Union Commission,* p. 4.

7. Hermann Sticher, "The Union of the Evangelical and Methodist Churches," p. 7.

8. Ibid., pp. 9–10.
9. Ibid., pp. 12–13.
10. Ibid., pp. 21–22.
11. Rudiger Minor, *Report on Church Union in East Germany,* p. 2.
12. William Nausner, "Be Eager to Maintain the Unity of the Spirit through the Bond of Peace," an address to the Central Conference of Central and Southern Europe, 1976, p. 7.
13. Sticher, "Union of Evangelical and Methodist Churches," p. 12.
14. Nausner, "Be Eager to Maintain the Unity," pp. 23–24.
15. Ibid., p. 27.
16. Ibid., p. 24.

12. Penultimate Conclusions

1. *The Discipline of The Methodist Church—1960,* pp. 1–2.
2. James K. Mathews, "Address to the Council of Bishops—1980."
3. *The Book of Discipline of The United Methodist Church—1972,* pp. 39–40.
4. Ibid., p. 44.
5. Ibid., p. 49.
6. Ibid., p. 69.
7. Ibid., p. 75.
8. Ibid., p. 82.
9. Ibid., pp. 83–84.
10. *Daily Christian Advocate—1972,* p. 223.
11. *The Book of Discipline of The United Methodist Church—1972,* p. 180.
12. *Daily Christian Advocate—1972,* p. 180.
13. Ibid., p. 182.
14. Ibid.
15. *The Book of Discipline of The United Methodist Church—1976,* p. 212.
16. *Daily Christian Advocate—1976,* pp. F 14–15.
17. Herbert Eckstein, "United Church, Renewed Church," from an address to the European Commission on Union.

Index